WALK TO THE WATER

A mountain walk along the Haute Route Pyrenees (HRP). From the Atlantic to the Mediterranean

Paul Robertson

Copyright © 2020 Paul Robertson

All rights reserved

All events that happened are true. Some of the names of people in the book have been changed to keep their anonymity.

No part of this book may be reproduced, or stored in a retrieval system, or transmitted in any form or by any means, electronic, mechanical, photocopying, recording, or otherwise, without express written permission of the publisher.

ISBN-13: 9798582278771
ISBN-10: 1477123456

Cover design by: Paul Robertson (Author)
Library of Congress Control Number: 2018675309

*For my Mother. Always with me
on every mountain top.*

Let's see colours that have never been seen
Let's go to places no one else has been

U2

Just a thought

Sat on a shelf in a discount book shop in the late nineteen eighties, a coffee table book called something like 'The Best Walks in the World Ever' catches my eye. I pick it up and thumb through its pages. I feel a surge of excitement having never seen half of the places listed before. Photographs of denim clad, bearded men wearing large framed rucksacks, surrounded by mountain peaks in exotic locations. The book evocatively lists multi day treks from all around the world, including Nepal, Pakistan, India, Peru, Europe, USA and New Zealand. Starting with the easiest and ending with the nearly impossible. Sitting somewhere near the back was the HRP, the mother of all hardship.

On the opening page for the Haute Randonnee Pyrenee chapter is a picture of Kev Reynolds wearing plus fours and great leather mountain boots, his shirt is undone to the navel and he may well have been wearing a medallion. He's on an impossibly steep slope as sun bleached mountains fade into the distance. It stuck in my mind, as did his route description. Forty days of wilderness, of toil through trackless terrain and camping high in the mountains miles from the nearest road. Written in the mid nineteen eighties, I guess it was like that, where boys leave home and if lucky, come back men. Unfortunately, 'The best walks in the world ever' got leant to someone or just plain disappeared a few years later. It didn't matter though as the HRP was forever etched in my mind.

I remember at the time thinking it all looked far too much like hard work but as the summers rolled past I saw other articles, books and maps. The Pyrenean beast had been tamed a little by the thoughtful French and Spanish with little blobs of paint and continuous track had started to form. By 2005 it was pretty much a marked route the whole way and I spent over two weeks walking just the middle bit.

I was hooked after that. The thought of walking through an ever changing landscape from one coast to another through a seemingly endless mountain range was always at the back of my mind. The ultimate prize for the mountain connoisseur, to complete the Haute Route Pyrenees. Having found myself between jobs and effectively homeless in 2014, the time had come. All I needed to do was undo my shirt to my navel and get a medallion..

The walk was a revelation, a once in a lifetime opportunity that came about during a happy period of my life. I never expected to walk it again five years later but life and circumstances threw up unquantifiable choices and I found myself staring at a blank page. I had to think it all up again, to find a reason to carry on. This book is that story.

Beginning

'You can't sleep here.'

A bald, shiny head in a white shirt, black trousers and steel toe cap boots is looking down at me and pointing to a sign.

'It says no camping, that means no lilos.'

'You're also a fire hazard. You'll have to go and sit over there.' And points to the world's most uncomfortable chair.

Staggering up, I deflate my thermarest and wonder if I'm about to burst into flames at any moment. I walk past the seats. I had marvelled earlier at this resurrected piece of medieval torture after trying to sit on it, every aspect of comfort has been stripped, leaving exposed metal and hard plastic.

If I can't lie down inside, I'll go outside then. By the entrance to

Arrivals, I see a spot behind a defunct bus shelter which is now a smoking point, so lay there for three hours on concrete. I'm curled in a ball on a small piece of foam from my backpack until the cold seeps into bones and cramp sets in. Wafts of cigarette smoke continually fill the air above.

Departures are now open, it's 3.30am and full of people. All the world's most uncomfortable chairs are taken. A couple are sat bolt upright, eyes closed in a sleep deprived coma in the corner, I'm so tired I crawl underneath them. No one says anything as I lay hidden by their suitcases.

'Alright Jim, I've signed the papers for the house and have moved out, the money goes through tomorrow. See you Tuesday.'

MESSAGE SENT. Beep!

Sun shines through the front window onto wooden floors, dust motes float in circles, refusing to land. It's a Thursday. I take a deep breath and sigh. The musty smell of the cellar mixed with a faint aroma of cigarettes is still here. Looking around, I gravitate to the kitchen and stare out the window. The garden's in full bloom, my mother's creation, her pride and joy.

She used to show me pictures of it whenever she visited.

'You're not looking Paul! I don't know why I bother.'

'I am! There's pink and yellow things, see.'

'Do you like it?'

'It's lovely Mum. Would you like another glass of wine?'

I find myself gripping the kitchen sink and lost in the past. I wish I could tell her how wonderful it all looks today but I can't. What was once a home is now a house, an empty shell. The nest has been stripped, sanitised and waits for the next owner to leave their mark. To fill it with laughter. And so it goes.

The front door swings shut. I feel myself welling up, the key is digging into my palm, I like the pain so squeeze it harder. Finally I let go and the key rattles through the letterbox, it puts up one last fight with the draught excluder and then clunks noisily as it hits the floor.

As I walk down the street, the imprint of the key in my palm slowly fades away and disappears.

RyanAir flight FR372 smacks down on the runway with all the usual no frills finesse. As we taxi, the pilot informs us.

'It's a balmy day out there, light winds and a scorching 38 degrees.'

Bodies clamber from seats, sweaty armpits and perfume waft in the air. A sea of elbows narrowly miss heads as heavy plastic cases are coaxed from overhead lockers. Mild cursing ensues and then a thump as a week's supply of underwear hits the floor. We shuffle though slowly, trying to avoid eye contact with the next row lest they squeeze in front. Nearly out and the air hostesses thank me for not buying one of their overpriced vile sandwiches. Standing on the runway, the heat makes me gasp, the air's so hot it's hard to swallow. I collect my bag and head outside.

Palm trees sway in the breeze, a deep blue sky above, Ooh la la, vive le France! I Switch on my phone and see there's a bus to Hendaye in twenty minutes so faff with Euros. I'm always amazed how quickly I forget the note denominations. As for the centimes? Still a mystery.

I hear an English voice in the distance.

'Yeah yeh, I'll be fine, dunno yet.... Not sure.... I ain't got a clue..... Better go.'

Andy, a pub landlord puts his phone down, lights a cigarette and has a mild look of terror on his face.

'Alrite Mate, what are you up to? You sound a little lost..'

'Oh thank God! An English man. Where is the bus stop? It's not very well sign-posted around here is it?'

'The bus stop's around the back I think. Where are you going?'

'I'm walking the Santiago de Compostela.'

Andy's face is bright red and puffed out from last night's celebrations. He lights another cigarette off the one he's just finishing and looks hopelessly out of shape.

'Well, there's a bus to Hendaye which I'm catching. From there I think you can get a bus or train to St Jean. Or if you like, you can walk with me for two days and then cut across to St Jean'

'That sounds great.' Andy eagerly replies.

On the bus, Andy tells me he needs to sort himself out. A heavy drinker, he wants to quit and sees the Compostela as the ideal opportunity.

'You see, it'll just be a few beers a night for the first week. Oh, they make a lovely Rioja so I'll have to have a few of them also but once I get into the swing of things I'll then give up.'

The bus pulls into Hendaye and it's a twenty minute walk to the beach. As we put on our packs, I can't help but notice a rather large bomb shaped cylinder strapped to Andy's pack.

'What's that thing?'

'Oh that's my Kelly Wood Cooker, for when I'm wild camping.'

As we walk, it swings from side to side as it's too big to fit in the pack. It's the most ridiculous contraption for backpacking I think I've ever seen, weighing more than two kilos.

'I think you should send it back, there's no wood where you're going anyway and it weighs a tonne.'

'I can't do that! My son bought it for me as a leaving present.'

As we near the beach, sweat runs off Andy's face and with every breath, he makes a weird coughing noise. I begin to question Andy's fitness and start doubting he'll make it up the first hill tomorrow, never mind Santiago.

'I'll be alright Paul, I walked up Maidstone high street the other day, that goes up alot. 600 metres I think.'

The beach at Hendaye is a mile or so long, the sun is setting as we walk to its far end. I can see a grassy platform which looks perfect for camping. It also has two naked men watching us approach. They stand, pot bellies sticking out, hands on hips and smiling at us, their little willies are semi erect.

'Did you see that Paul?' Andy shouts .

'Yep, they seem to like the look of you.'

Tents are up and it's getting dark. We sit outside supping beer and watching storm clouds as they fill the horizon. The fat, naked men are gone, now three cheeky chaps in their thirties are walking around our grassy patch. They seem to be looking for something. They file past one at a time, smile and then disappear into the darkness. On cue, a full moon rises and a few more men appear.

Now all together, it's starting to get rather noisy at the other end of the grassy patch. The wind is picking up and a gust then bellows in. A bright white flash followed by a thunder clap. The rain falls heavily as lots of french cursing has replaced the rhythmic grunting. They pull on clothes and run down the beach..

Rain and wind rattles the flysheet as I lay inside. My phone rings.

'Alrite Jim, nice to see you brought the weather with you!'

'Just got to the beach. Where are you?'

"When you see some half naked men running past you - look for a grassy patch.'

'Err OK'.

I float in the sea, the swell lifts me up and down. Staring at the Cloudless sky, I let go. I feel myself being sucked up into the blue. My head is a ball of grief, the last eighteen months have stripped any reason I once had. I feel empty and alone. Up and down I float like a feather launched into the sky. With my eyes closed, it feels like I'm racing towards a deep black void..

Then.

THUMP!

Water goes up my nose as I tumble in the wave that breaks over me and I get washed up near the shore.

Across the beach where the tents were pitched, there's a shout.

'Come on Paul, stop dicking around.'

Andy having breakfast.

* * *

ROLLING THROUGH THE BASQUE COUNTY

Lone donkey at Azekerreta

One

The morning is a confusion of shops. One supermarket doesn't have all we need so we head to another. As per usual, I have bought too much and can't get it all in without a fight. The six baguettes sitting on top already resemble Pitta breads. Andy, being much more resourceful, decides to just put his food in a massive carrier bag. His R2D2 size Cooker now sits proudly on the top of his rucksack leaving no room for anything much else. He's also wearing some kind of leather Stetson which has all the ventilation of a bin bag and seems to be gently boiling his brain.

'I'll pack it later.' He mutters, shifting the bag from one hand to the other.

Just when it looks as though we might actually get going, there's a look of panic on Jim's face. 'I need some cigarettes and the Tabac's shut down.'

'I'm down to my last two packs.' Andy realises.

We weave our way through town, it's Tabacless. It's also eleven am by now and getting very hot.

Jim pronounces to Andy. ' We'll have to walk to Spain.'

Bags are dumped under a tree and I sit guarding them on a shady bench. I dream idly of ice creams and ponder the virtues of walking back to the beach for a siesta. Forty minutes later and I spot Jim in the distance. Andy's around 100 metres behind him and is walking like he just shat his pants.

'I can't go on, I'll have to go back'. Andy winces upon arrival.

'You can't go back, we haven't got anywhere yet to go back from'.

I helpfully tell him.

'What's up?'

'My feet are killing me, it's these boots, they no longer fit. I don't understand..'

Andy's feet were swollen. The combination of too much of a good time, the heat and a run to Spain and back has finished him off. I look at his bare feet, they are puffed up like pain aux chocolates, unfortunately they don't smell the same.

'You need some running trainers, something with lots of mesh, there's a Decathlon in town. While you're at it, go to the post office and send back your cooker and boots.'

'Sorry lads, I'm going to find a hotel. I'll have to buy some trainers I think and try again tomorrow. Catch a bus to St Jean.. Anyone want a carrier bag of food?'

By now it's nearly noon, we all shake hands and Andy turns to head back to the seafront. He looks quite chipper considering and gives me his milk powder as a parting gift.

'Think I might go for a pint before the hotel,' are his parting words. I feel overwhelmingly sad for him. He's a really nice bloke.

So three have now become two.

'Shall we go out into the midday sun like mad dogs?"

'Yes...' Jim replies. 'I really thought he would have lasted more than two miles.'

'Come on, we best get a move on before it cools down.'

The route out of Hendaye climbs steadily through boulevards before connecting with a series of dirt roads and tracks through open countryside. Once past the motorway, we encounter our first rolling green hill. There's no wind and it's unbearably hot. The path contours around Choldokogagna. We hit patches of woodland but there's little shade. From Col d'Oslin the path leads to a highpoint. I collapse under a tree and try and suck out the last of the water vapour in my bottle.

'My pack is killing me Jim, I think I'm too old for this shit.'

I look at my rucksack, it's bursting with food. There's only one thing for it so I start digging out its contents and sort out a pile of the extra food I can live without. Half a kilo of cheese, 700 grams of muesli, a box of couscous, a tray of brownies, a pack of biscuits and a box of milk powder (some people are so ungrateful), placing it all in front of me, I start unwrapping. The cheese has already magically turned into yogurt and the chocolate brownies look like the after effects of a dodgy stomach. It's all tipped into a nearby ditch and I kick some dirt over it. A nice treat for the worms I think to myself as the wrappers are stuffed back in the pack. I put the rucksack back on, it still feels the same. Bollox.

We head over the mighty Col d'Mandale at 573 metres and cross open moorland. The path now contours around the next hill. I can hear water, I'm sure of it. Has a dehydrated madness entered my head? Rounding a corner and there it is, a small gurgling spring.

'Woo hooo!' I holler and neck a litre. I take off my shirt and put it in the muddy puddle underneath the spring and then throw water all over myself like a demented baby elephant.

A small bush offers some shade. Sitting under it, I watch Jim stagger around the corner.

'I can't go on, it's too bloody hot.'

'Stick your head in there, you'll be alright in five minutes.'

'I've had enough, I'm going to camp in those trees over there.'

'Can't do that Jim, we've only been walking for three hours. Have a fag.'

'Fuck that, I'm having two.'

Twenty minutes and possibly three cigarettes later, Jim starts to feel semi normal again. Passing through some pines and across a mini plateau, we arrive at a bluff above a row of ugly new supermarkets that are sat on the open hillside straddling the French/Spanish border. A path drops to a tarmac road passing glass fronted shops all selling the same cheap plonk and spirits. They seem deserted apart from a retired couple pushing a trolley around. It's empty but for a bottle of absinthe and eggnog sat at the bottom of it.

Cloud covers the sun mercifully as the road crossing of Col d'Ibardin is reached. A small lane is followed and then dirt tracks. La Rhune towers overhead, its radio mast looks like a rocket ship and gives the hill the look of something out of Thunderbirds.

'I'm not going over that.'

'Nope, neither am I Jim.'

I'd been over it five years before so it didn't really bother me. I was also standing at the same spot four hours earlier, so knew there wasn't enough time even if I wanted to.

The track carries on and passes through some pines, someone is packing a rucksack ahead of us. As we draw closer, a tall Moroccan guy as skinny as a beanpole is standing, grinning at us.

'Hey guys, what are you doing walking in this heat, you must be fucking mad!'

He had a point. Majeed stuffs the last of his belongings into his pack and joins us as we carry on.

'You gotta start at five in morning Man, walk until eleven then sleep til five and then walk until eleven.'

He rabbits on and then looks up at La Rhune. 'There's no way I'm going up there, fucking madness!'

And so two become three again as we drop downhill and hit the road for the final five kilometres. It climbs cruelly up and Jim drops behind. Majeed is just in front and is glistening with sweat. There's a smell I recognise from my college days in the air, it's marijuana. I think I'm imagining things and then wonder if it's perhaps growing by the roadside. I then realise it's actually coming from Majeed. He is sweating pure THC. We have just bumped into a man who is basically a walking cannabis plant.

Finally we arrive at Lizuniaga, a restaurant/bar on the Spanish border. Jim and Majeed go and get a drink. I know that if I have a beer now, I'll just collapse under the nearest tree for the night, so put up my tent and walk up the road to a font with a wooden trough. Stripping off to the waist, I lather up with soap. Foam oozes out of the front of my shorts as I have a rummage. Turning around to wash my back, I look across at a house opposite and notice for the first time, a family of eight people sitting outside. They've stopped eating mid mouthful and are staring at me as I foam gently.

'Hola!' I shout across, sploshing water down my shorts. 'Lovely day!'

Nobody answers so I quickly gather my bits and head to the tent and then the bar.

I find Jim and Majeed quite easily, they are the only people there. Majeed has a plate of chicken casserole in front of him and is chewing on a chicken leg. Jim looks up like a dying man who has just been given his last rites.

We sup beer and Majeed enviably skins up.

Jim looks at me and finishes his beer. I'm off to bed he states, with a look of mild panic. I stick around, I always fancied myself as a hard core toker in my youth so couldn't really pass up on some proper Moroccan hash. I have two tokes, pass it back and then have two more. Majeed is now in full flow, telling me how he is Berber and not an Arab, how Berbers are the oldest human race in the world.

I feel good.

I feel great.

Ooh.. not too sure now.

I feel my world start to spin.

Majeed starts to skin up again. I make my excuses and we arrange to meet again in two days. His route goes a different way to ours but we'll cross paths then. I weave my way back to the tent and then cling on to my thermarest for the next half hour until a fudge like sleep envelopes.

Jim

I first met Jim five years ago at Lizuniaga, so it seems apt to introduce him now.

Having started from Hendaye then at the more motivated time of nine in the morning, it was a wholly different first day. The rain poured in a monsoon intensity. I fell in line with James, another HRP'er (more on him later), so we teamed up for the day and squelched our way over La Rhune and down to the restaurant at Lizuniaga. Whilst putting up our tents, Jim appears, having also started the HRP that day, proudly stating how he cheated and skipped La Rhune. He had the look of a mad man and I liked him immediately. He then disappeared into the bar and I joined him half an hour later.

He was sitting at a table with a massive plate of poussin legs and chips in front of him. There must have been a dozen legs at least.

'Here, have some.'

'I didn't know chickens in France were so closely related to centipedes?'

We sit and chat.' I don't have any maps, I'm just using the guide book.' I found this quite intriguing, having gone for many walks with a map but no guide book - I never thought of trying it the other way. I mean why would I? It's just plain bonkers.

'You'll get giddy you know.'

'Why's that?'

'Because when the Basque fog descends you'll spend all day going around in circles.'

'Hmm, another chicken leg Paul?'

The following morning James and I set off but yesterday's enthusiasm has worn off and he's as stiff as a board. After a few hours James declares he needs a siesta and crawls under a tree. In the distance I can see Jim and soon catch him up. He is faithfully following the guidebook. It's nestled in the palm of his hand, thumb on the right page. Then as if on cue the stars align, a cloud rolls in covering the hillside.

'This way.' I confidently state.

We follow a ridge line, after a while it becomes apparent it's the wrong ridge line. A river runs below so it seems like a good idea to follow that and intersect the ridge that we should have been on later. Unfortunately, the river disappears into a thick impenetrable scrub. Admitting defeat we turn around. I then narrowly miss standing on a snake curled up in the thick heather as we end up back where we started.

Jim sits down and makes a cigarette. 'Good these maps aren't they?' He quips.

I notice on his leg, a tick and then another. It turns out we were both covered in them so start pulling them off in a mild panic.

'Jim pull down your shorts, they'll be buried in your chappy before you know it. They like it warm and hot.'

He does so and then turns around whilst I made sure there were none on his arse. I turned around and drop my shorts .

'Any on me?'

'Nope,' came a distant reply. I turn and see him facing the other way making another cigarette.

'What about my ticks?'

'They won't touch that.'

Heading on down the ridge I see James in the distance shouting obscenities at a fence blocking his way, for he too has gone the wrong way. The three of us eventually get back on track and walk on to Azikun, a lovely quaint village. An old bar beckons us in. As we enter it's as if time has stood still. Apart from a newish TV, the place looks like something from the 1950's. A ninety year old lady serves us beer. James says he has to phone his buddy who is running his radio station for him and is about to go live on air. Jim and I sit as James answers questions about the walk so far. A song is put on after the interview.

'Gosh James are you famous.. Where are you broadcasting to?

'Well it's my radio station, I do it for fun.'

There's a moment of silence. OK I'll be honest I only have a following of around twenty people!'

The next day I head into France to buy food, as I'd originally planned on walking the first week on the GR10 and Jim and James carry on the HRP. I rejoin it three days later, bored of my own company and successfully intersect with Jim. James has dropped out as his feet are mincemeat. Jim and I then walk for the next month together. It works out just fine, Jim admits that maps are useful after all and I get to smoke his fags whenever I drink too much red wine. Perfect. And that is how I met Jim.

Jim thinking about having a cigarette, whilst having a cigarette

Two

5 am and there's a rustling noise nearby and mild cursing.. More rustling.. A torch beam scours the horizon and Majeed is gone. I do the decent thing and go back to sleep.

Jim and I set off at 9 am, 'well it's 8 am in England Jim, so that's plenty early enough.' I reason with him.

It's a plod up the dirt road, elevated above the valley, distant green hills merge into the coastal heat haze.

'This is like Wales.' I exclaim.

'You said that yesterday.'

'I'll probably say it tomorrow.....And the next.'

After an hour and a half of passing through pleasant pastureland, Col de Lizarreta is reached. A cafe sits just below so I head in. A rather attractive lady smiles as I enter.

'Hola.'

'Ah your English, what is your name?'

'Paul.. Paulo. And yours?'

'Maria.'

Maria's dark curly hair is tied loosely back, her blue eyes twinkle. She is quite gorgeous.

'You like the Basque country'

Yes. Very much.'

'It's very beautiful here, maybe you like it so much you will stay a while…'

'Err. I certainly could, I've nothing really pressing on right now.'

'Here. Look at this picture. It's my grandfather.'

The picture is of a man taken in the 1960's. He's up a tower waving what looks like a massive butterfly net over his head.

'He's catching birds as they migrate through the pass, it's a very old custom here. It's how we used to feed our families.'

I look at her neck as she speaks, a lock of hair loosely brushes it.

'Yep. I could do that if you like?'

'Haha! There's not enough now. Now we shoot them!'

'Let me teach you some of the Basque language, it's a very old language, one of the oldest in the world.'

I look at the bar and wonder which room above it will be ours. I have to break the news to Jim that I'm going no further. He's carrying the maps this time so will manage. He'll understand when he sees her. If not, fuck him.

'Egun on izan dezala.' It means. ' Have a nice day.'

'It sounds a little like Welsh..' . I start to say when an equally handsome man walks into the room.

'Ah look, here is my husband. Pedro.'

'Well of course it is.'

Stone

'Mae hin ddistaw iawn yma hebddo chi'

'Are you sure that's right? I mean if we get this wrong it could be really bad'

'Martin's adamant.' My sister replies. 'He is Welsh, so he should know! `

I read it out again.

'Mae hin ddistaw iawn yma hebddo chi' . ' It's very quiet now you're gone'. 'OK, I'm just paranoid it could be interpreted as 'It's very quiet down here.'

'Are you OK brother?'

'No, not really, I miss her terribly.'

'Me too.'

I put down the phone and fill out the form to send back to the stonemasons. It's been four months already. They promise the gravestone will be in place by Christmas.

'Where have you been?' Jim asks impatiently as I bring out two luke warm coffees.

'Just learning another language.'

Maria comes out and clears the table next to ours.

'Ohh.. I see now.'

The path now drops down through trees, across a stream then climbs back up to more high rolling tops.Dirt roads interlink and then it's a pull up to Col Bagacheta and we leave the GR11. Once more in cloud, navigation this time is much easier as all the maps are on my phone. It feels like I'm cheating as it takes out all the guesswork but the right ridge is followed this time descending to the small hamlet of Azpikueta. I pick some plums, they're delicious so scoff four or five. I then notice small holes in all the remaining plums that I have just put in a bag, each hole has a maggot in it. All of a sudden I'm not so hungry.

The wind starts picking up and the sky darkens, a flash, a distant rumble. We look for likely camping spots but it's all far too rural. Upon entering the village of Azikun, the rain starts to pour. It's still as quaint and unspoiled as the last time so dash into the same bar where we were once on the radio.. This too is the same but a younger old lady now resides behind it. I ask if the older old lady is still with us.

'Ah yes, mumma still likes to help when we need her, though these big glasses you English like to drink from are too heavy for her to pick up!'

The rain continues to pour, bouncing outside off the pavement. The not so old, old lady asks if we'd like to stay in her Pension. We look at each other and then look again at the street as the gutters overflow.

'Another beer then Jim? We are on holiday after all.'

Basque hills above Azpikueta

Three

I leave the room and light my cooker under the veranda outside on the pavement. It's still raining and a low cloud shrouds the hills. The village is waking up and people walk past looking at the strange foreigner who's too tight to buy a coffee across the road.

A concrete track heads out of Arizkun, the rain has stopped but the cloud still seems full of it. I consult the map, as usual it shows comically little detail so I switch on the phone. It's map shows a turn off in a hundred metres.

'See that neck height bracken over there Jim? That's the way apparently.'

'Of course it is.' Jim then rolls a cigarette whilst looking at the jungle ahead. 'That stuff can give you cancer you know.' As he inhales deeply.

'Maybe you should stick to Golden Virginia. Much safer.'

I wade in first, there's a path of sorts underneath. The bracken is soaking and very soon we are dripping wet. The path is lost but the phone says otherwise so we continue up, eventually onto the hillside and to Azekerreta. A forlorn looking donkey is watching us from its shed and makes no effort to investigate. We obviously look like no hopers on the carrot front.

A four wheel drive track is then followed as I try to make sense of the guide book. Jim gets out the map.

'This map is rubbish, there's no donkey on it.'

'No mention of donkeys by Tonni either.'

Ton Joosten's guide book, The Pyrenean Haute Route, became a source of much ridicule on the first HRP crossing. At times it can be at best described as confusing. "After 2 kms you meet the GR11 coming in from the right. Don't turn right but keep following the dirt road that bends to the left". Or. "ignore the dirt road to your right and follow the dirt road" It didn't help that the only time we'd look at the guide book was when a wrong turning was made or a junction was reached that wasn't on the map. The maps of course were another story. At least Tonni tried to make sense of his surroundings. Spanish cartographers were slapdash at best. Twenty metre contour lines gave most of the hills the appearance of sand dunes, cliffs gleefully ignored. GR routes were coloured in as if done by a five year old at art class, no doubt with a felt pen grasped in the palm of the hand, tongue sticking out of the side of the mouth. It did add to the feeling of adventure being mildly lost but sometimes you just want to get to where you're going.

'OK let's cheat, it's that way according to the phone'. We follow a succession of tracks zigzagging through the mist and eventually end up at a wooded escarpment. The path up Burga hill then disappears, it's buried under leaves. No one else goes up here except HRP loonies I surmise. We eventually find the top and sit looking at the thick fog as it swirls around our ankles. The guide book extols its fine views.

Spooky goings on below Burga hill

'Probably just looks like Wales, come on let's get out of here.' We head down and more confusion of criss crossing tracks later, the village of Les Aldudes is seen through a gap in the mist below. Once out of the gloom the track cuts down the hillside. It starts to rain so I run on ahead and stop under a building's veranda and wait for Jim.

'PAUL!, PAUL!'

I look up and see Majeed high on the facing hillside waving at me like he's about to set sail on the Titanic. We greet each other like long lost buddies, Mahjeed is laughing hysterically and his eyes are so wide open I fear they may fall out of his head. He gives the impression he may have lost the plot at some point in our absence. Sitting outside a cafe and wedged under an umbrella I look at Mahjeed's rucksack properly for the first time.

'What's in there?' I point to a strange protruding lump in an outside pocket.

'Oh that's my drone. I carry it everywhere, It's amazing brother, you gotta get one. I'll show you some footage later. It only weighs two kilos.'

The garage down the road allows camping behind it for free, I head into its shop to see if they have any treats. Inside is a full blown supermarket.

'Jim why are we carrying eight days food from Hendaye when we could have bought five days worth from here?'

'Erm, I forgot'.

We disappear into our tents once up as the rain is still pouring. Armed with wine and crisps I see no reason to leave again until the morning.

'PAUL! Open your door brother!' I do so and a small white missile comes flying in. I ignore it for a while, I'm enjoying my wine but in the end I crack. Just a puff, I tell myself. An evening of clinging to the thermarest ensues...

I awake and rain is still drumming on the tent roof. We all agree moving is pointless. Wafts of marijuana float past all morning. By lunchtime cabin fever starts to set in. Mahjeed is playing Fleetwood Mac and seems to be giggling at nothing in particular. I go across and sit in his tent porch .

'Brother. I am really stoned.'

' I'm not surprised, that stuff is lethal. It's so strong.'

'No way man! It's good for you, look at me.. HA HA HA!!

'Would you like some, here take some man. I have plenty.'

I see a Tupperware box at the bottom of the tent. He must have half a kilo of the stuff. It's white and crystallized. I've never seen such a bad ass looking skunk.

'Maybe later, thanks though.'

I toke on a spliff he's smoking and then pretend I've gotta do something urgently in my tent.

I do as a matter of fact, it's called lying down.

'PAUL! HA HA !! Open your door!'

Another missile flies in. I've been asleep for two hours after my earlier visit.

'Thanks buddy.' I shout back.

Little do I know that's the last time I'll see him. Just as well, in hindsight.

Four

5am. Rustle, rustle, flap, flap. A flash of torchlight and he's gone.

The cloud is so low it's hurting my head this morning.. Well, something is. After packing we head to the cafe, it's an excuse to delay leaving but one we both embrace. We dig out the map and guidebook to check what pain the day has to offer.

'Tonni says mist will make navigation very difficult, especially on the first part of the day'

'There's another route Jim'. We can head up the valley and miss the first two tops. And rejoin it here'. I say pointing at the map.

Jim agrees. To be honest, if it involves missing a hill or two he always agrees. If I said to him let's go mountaineering in East Anglia he'd readily agree to that too. For an hour, a small country lane is followed passing pleasant little hamlets as farming folk go about their business, an old drovers track branches off to the left disappearing up into the cloud and a small stream is crossed.

'Can you remember where the next water is Jimmy?'

'Church on the pass above Roncesvalles I believe'

OK I'll grab a couple of litres here, it looks like the sun's trying to come out.'

The track is beautiful, it winds up slowly and having already avoided two hills there's no great rush, the cloud starts breaking up and the view of intersecting valleys fade into the distant Les Aldudes. After a couple of hours, Col d' Hauzay at the heady height of 965 metres is reached and a tarmac cross roads.

' I stopped up on that bank last time, I think we should do it again so I can have fag.'

'Jim, there's a tap here, why have I just carried two kilos of water up here?'

'Oh, so there is.'

I tip one litre of water away. From here it's a small tarmac road all the way to Col de Roncesvalles and its church. We're now walking close to the border and Limoux, a small hill pokes above the trees on our right ,

'HRP goes over that, shall we?'

'No thanks'

A group of cyclist's wizz past and I'm slightly envious as a steep drop down to Col du Roncesvalles has the knees pounding and feet slapping on its tarmac slopes. The church has everything you'd expect from something built in the early seventies, it's ugly, has no character and will probably fall down soon. It stands on the pass like something Batman would sit on to watch over Gotham City below.

'If you go inside, it has nice windows, ahh the doors are locked.' I hear Jim shout as I look for water. There's no tap. Today is the last time I have to rely on Jim's amazing ability to forget anything useful, as I rejoined the HRP a few hours from this point on the previous crossing. I rejoice at the thought. A steady climb follows, we are now on the Santiago de Compostela and the last of the day's pilgrims are slowly making their way down and past us.

'Bonka Meenoo!'

'Bonka Meenoo!'

The exchange makes me smile, though I'm sure the novelty must wear thin by the time you get to Santiago. Some are more enthusiastic than others, one guy with long hair in particular looks quite out of it. He's grinning insanely as he walks past. We both agree he must have just had lunch with Majeed. I walk on and wonder what happened to Andy, hoping we'll bump into him on the off chance. Alas not. A font is reached and I take a long drink having run out of water earlier.

'We turn off at a font don't we?'

'It's the next one.' Jim replies.

I'm tired and too lazy to look at the map, it seems an easy junction to follow so we head off knowing the day is nearly over. The mist is thick and cool, we're trundling along downhill and busily thinking about nothing when a tarmac road suddenly appears.

'There is no other font... Where's the font? Where's the font .. Jim?'

I sound and feel mildly demented, probably not that dissimilar to John Cleese in Fawlty Towers.

'We'll have to head back up, maybe there was only one.' Manuel replies.

'Oh bugger that.'

I'm now on familiar ground, I followed this road before when I rejoined the HRP last time so suggest we walk along it to the border and camp. The road is longer than I remember, it's then uphill to my camping spot, but there's no water. Just oozing mud where cattle have scanked and shat in the waters souce. Next to it is a flat green fenced off enclosure near a tree plantation, it's ideal for the night. Once the tents are up we head west in a quest to find the first and only font. Within two minutes we are there, a mere two hours after leaving it the first time. We look at each other and laugh, well you have to really.

Heading back, the cloud lifts. Urculu's escarpment fills the western horizon. A light mist clings to its crown, its slopes have an uncanny resemblance to Pen y Fan, it's a comforting sight as darkness falls.

Urculu

Funeral

'Are you sure you're Okay Paul?'

Ian our Celebrant touches my shoulder as I look across the small gathering in front.

'Yes I think so.. Thank you.' I take a deep breath and start to read.

Mum absolutely loved the Brecon Beacons. My first recollection of this was as a youngster on family trips to Aberporth to see my grandparents. The route there always went past the Brecon Beacons to which Mum would exclaim.

'I've never seen anything like it.' As they came into view.

As the years went on, the hills became more of a focal point whenever Amanda, Mum and I would get together. We would go out walking as a threesome and would debate over and over again which hills were the best. It was always the same on top, flasks of coffee, probably the best homemade Welsh cakes in the world and a view that normally consisted of cloud and drizzle. It didn't matter though because whichever way we looked

'I've never seen anything like it.' Would always be heard.

In the last few days, Amanda and I did a kind of 'tribute walk' up Pen y Fan. We took a lock of mum's hair so she could be with us one more time to her favourite of all favourite views . We released it to the wind and it shot up high into the air only to then drop just below us on a grassy ledge. I don't think she wanted to go too far just yet so we could all be together one last time. We drank coffee and ate far inferior shop bought Welsh cakes.

The only thing missing this time was the immortal words

'I've never seen anything like it'.

Because there was nothing like my mum.

I look up relieved the ordeal is over. There's a few smiles as silence once more envelopes the room. Outside the sun is shining, our little procession makes its way through the graveyard. We cast posies of flowers picked from the garden, onto the coffin. Everyone is dressed in a floral tribute, bright colors, anything with flowers. An attempt to brighten the darkest day of my life. My uncle is wearing a Hawaiian shirt and unexpectedly starts to sing in Welsh. His voice is strong and direct. What I have left holding myself together crumbles as I listen.

> Paham mae dicter, O Myfanwy,
> Yn llenwi'th lygaid duon di?
> A'th ruddiau tirion, O Myfanwy,
> Heb wrido wrth fy ngweled i?
> Pa le mae'r wên oedd ar dy wefus
> Fu'n cynnau 'nghariad ffyddlon ffôl?
> Pa le mae sain dy eiriau melys,
> Fu'n denu'n nghalon ar dy ôl?
> Pa beth a wneuthum, O Myfanwy
> I haeddu gwg dy ddwyrudd hardd?
> Ai chwarae oeddit, O Myfanwy
> Â thanau euraidd serch dy fardd?
> Wyt eiddo im drwy gywir amod
> Ai gormod cadw'th air i mi?
> Ni cheisiaf fyth mo'th law, Myfanwy,
> Heb gael dy galon gyda hi.
> Myfanwy boed yr holl o'th fywyd
> Dan heulwen ddisglair canol dydd.
> A boed i rosyn gwridog iechyd
> I ddawnsio ganmlwydd ar dy rudd.
> Anghofia'r oll o'th addewidion
> A wnest i rywun, 'ngeneth ddel,
> A dyro'th law, Myfanwy dirion
> I ddim ond dweud y gair "Ffarwél"

> Why is it anger, O Myfanwy,
> That fills your eyes so dark and clear?

> Your gentle cheeks, O sweet Myfanwy,
> Why blush they not when I draw near?
> Where is the smile that once most tender
> Kindled my love so fond, so true?
> Where is the sound of your sweet words,
> That drew my heart to follow you?
> What have I done, O my Myfanwy,
> To earn your frown? What is my blame?
> Was it just play, my sweet Myfanwy,
> To set your poet's love aflame?
> You truly once to me were promised,
> Is it too much to keep your part?
> I wish no more your hand, Myfanwy,
> If I no longer have your heart.
> Myfanwy, may you spend your lifetime
> Beneath the midday sunshine's glow,
> And on your cheeks O may the roses
> Dance for a hundred years or so.
> Forget now all the words of promise
> You made to one who loved you well,
> Give me your hand, my sweet Myfanwy,
> But one last time, to say "farewell".

Five

I open the tent door to cloudless skies. The hills stretch off into the distance, a series of green escarpments folding into the blue horizon. Trees fill the valleys to our south in Spain, open grazed bare slopes to the North fall into the mists of France. We're camped on a high ridge, so most of the day's efforts are behind us. Passing under the slopes of Urculu the day begins, a series of animal tracks cut across the hill side and a minor road is reached after an hour. We walk on to a view point and look at the road threading its way across the high moorland ahead.

'Today looks quite easy Jim.'

'Oh good, time for a cigarette then'. We sit down, content in the warm glow of not having to do so much today.

'There is of course that hill near the end of the day that almost made you vomit last time.'

'That's tomorrow isn't it?'

'No that's the other horrendous one, this is the one we took a shortcut on and you took so long getting up it I boiled water and made you a coffee whilst waiting.'

'I think I'll just have one cigarette for now.'

The road makes for mindless miles, it stays high offering distant views. A junction is reached and we drop down to a stream to have lunch on a bridge. The day has been pretty hot and sweaty so I strip off and jump in. Horse flies appear from nowhere and start biting, I try to wash with one hand whilst swatting and cursing with the other.

'Ahh, Ow! Bloody things!'

'Bon Jour!'

Out of nowhere a French couple appear and walk over the bridge.

I turn around in surprise and give them a full frontal.

'Oh.. Hi!'

They keep walking and don't stop. I'm not surprised.

We walk over to the slope of doom, this time taking the longer route that starts further down the valley. The path climbs steeply and is no wider than 12 inches, it zigzags across the face of the hillside all the way to the top. Half way up, I'm distracted by the view and walk off the path. Luckily my one knee wedges between some tussocks and I grab a tuft of grass with the other. The river's far below and I'd have cart wheeled all the way down into it. I'm in no doubt that it would have been quite painful.

Reaching the top, Jim soon follows.

'Not so bad.' He retorts, stroking his beard

I look at him and think, has he got fitter or am I just older? I lament my loss of superiority.

'Ah I remember now, you're not carrying all that shite are you?'

'What do you mean?'

I start listing the contents of his rucksack the first time around. 'The wooden pepper grinder, the full shaving kit (Jim has a beard), the kilo of brown sugar, the boot polish and brushes, the kilo of sultanas!'

'Yep, that could be it. Or maybe you're just turning into an old wanker.'

Pleasantries over, we cross over the pass. Cloud thickens and it looks like a storm is imminent. Dropping down to the twisting stream bed in a steep sided valley we look for somewhere to camp. Cattle are down below, so we find a flat spot just big enough between the dried out cow pats and get the tents up.

The evening is spent listening to distant thunder and trying not to think too much about flash floods.

Six

We pack in the morning under leaden skies, there's a break or two but it's not hopeful. A short walk follows the road and then we're confronted by a wall of grass. Just as we are about to set off, a young couple walk towards us asking the way to France. They're backpacking but look more like they should be heading to Glastonbury than the high hills. After much pointing and a detailed route description they thank me and walk in the opposite direction.

'No! It's that way!' I shout.

They just wave and carry on walking.

'Maybe they didn't want to go to France, they only asked where it was' Jim quips.

We look again at the hill. 'Right ho, let's go!'

It's a fairly relentless climb, Jim keeps up with me which I obviously find annoying. As we near the top we are once again in thick mist. The wind picks up and for the first time, waterproofs are put on as it drizzles. A faint track follows the ridge line, there's a strong smell of ammonia as the top is neared, over a hundred sheep welcome us bleating manically at 1333 metres. Some run to the cliff edge but stop. They may only have the brain the size of walnut but they're not that stupid.

We carry on up and over another hill on the ridge, eventually dropping down to the Col Curutche. The mist is really thick now and the drizzle turns to rain. The high plateau has some dolmans on it and stone circles somewhere but it's cold and wet and well, we don't really give two shits.

The path then drops though woodland and eventually we stumble out onto a road. The rain is still pouring so we duck into a refuge. We are now back in France and on the GR10 once more.

After two coffees at extortionate French prices it's time to head off, the rain has eased and the wind's picked up. I stop to take off my waterproofs, two lads in their early 20's walk past and I spot they're English. Andy and John are at university together. I fall in line with them and we chat whilst going up hill, they keep up a cracking pace whilst jabbering on. I pretend I have to look at something in my pack and stop. I watch them disappear around the corner and hear Jim's words from yesterday echo around my head.

'Maybe you're just turning into an old wanker.'

An afternoon of forested hills follows, there's little point in dallying so I push on to the nonsense that is Iraty. Luckily there's not much to see as the cloud has dropped again. Iraty is a ski village. Or it wants to be a ski village but seems to have little to offer other than a tourist office with an attached shop selling local delicacies.There may be more to it somewhere but I never found it last time and wasn't too fussed to look now. I wait by some old triangular ski chalets, they are pointy and tall like a witch's hat. There's a pack of dried apricots still unopened in my food bag, I grab a handful, fully aware of their sulfuric powers should you overindulge and look forward to the results tomorrow, preferably a few steps in front of Jim .

'Like an apricot?'

'Rude not to...Oh look , they've built a new hideous glass visitors centre just for us, shall we go and have a closer look.'

We enter the shop and wince at the prices, a young woman is sat behind the till idly playing with her phone.

'Are you bored?' I ask, more to satisfy my boredom than hers

'No.'

'Liar!'

She giggles and I ask where they are hiding the cheap wine.

'This wine is good, it's organic.'

'It's also twelve euros a bottle.'

'We have nothing for people like you, I am sorry.'

Jim takes no notice and is on a mission scouring the shelves. He has the look of a man who needs a drink. 'Paul, I've found one that's ten euros, shall we?'

'Do people like me drink this one?' I ask at the till.

'No, they normally bring their own up here!'

We leave the shop armed with our very expensive plonk.

'She was nice.'

'Well Jim, considering the only other females we've seen today were standing in their own piss and thinking of jumping off a cliff rather than be close to us, I guess you could say that.'

'I'd say she's the most beautiful girl in Iraty'

'She's the only girl in Iraty!'

We stand fumbling with our rucksacks wondering what to do next.

'Hello'

The most beautiful girl in Iraty is stood in front of us.

'You can go inside the tourist office if you wish, it's nice and warm in there and you can enjoy local wine in comfort. There's also a kitchen if you need it'

'Merci a vous.' Jim coo's. 'See.'

'OK, I agree, she is the most beautiful girl in Iraty, let's get inside.'

The kitchen is warm so we sit for an hour sipping our wine slowly as we're definitely not buying another one. It's quite an odd set up, there's a few walkers in here and a Gypsy family cooking a four course meal in the corner. Everyone looks bored and unsure what to do next so I take solace that it's not just me. We then debate whether five euros for half a bottle of wine each is a better value. It's getting late now so head up the hill behind Iraty armed with six litres of water each and camp just below some shooting huts in the fog, hoping for better weather in the morning.

Dawn over Pic d'Orchy

Seven

It's early, the sun is low and Pic d'Orchy is looking resplendent bathed in golden light. Fog fills the valleys below as we head towards our first 2000 metre peak. Jim seems quite tired today so I take full advantage and walk on ahead to make him feel worse. A number of small hills are crossed before the main climb starts. Half way up there's a big notch taken out of the ridge line, some kind of geological fault. I tried scrambling across it last time and nearly came a cropper. I look behind and see Jim in the distance, he's definitely struggling. There seems little point waiting here so I climb down around it and push on to the top.

Vultures circle overhead probably trying to work out if the scrawny wee man half way up is worth the effort of landing nearby, they don't, there's obviously bigger fish to fry. As I reach the top, it's covered in walkers of all shapes and sizes, a bit of a shock after the last few days having hardly seen a soul. I sit and wait for half an hour, the views are as remembered, quite spectacular. The high Pyrenees are in the distance, peaks at around 2500 metres line the horizon. In the near distance the rest of our route snakes towards them. Sticking to around 1800 metres, we'll be following the crest of the hills for the rest of the day.

'Yep, that's how I remember it. Bastard hill.'

'Only a few more to go Jimmy.' As I point into the far distance.

'Oh good.' Jim kicks off his boots and slowly eats lunch. I'm ready to go by now but I fear he may strangle me if I suggest so. Half an hour later we head down to the road where all the odd shaped people have parked their cars and continue along the Frontier ridge. The path is marked by pegs and is a delight to follow as it skirts around the unnecessary tops. Cloud blows in and out shrouding the views every now and again but at least it keeps the worst of the sun off us. The rounded hills now end and a more mountainous proposition lies ahead. I stop and wait, sitting on my pack, I watch an inversion bubble up from the French lowlands. It threatens to mask the rest of the day but instead creeps through the Cols leaving the tops sticking out like fantastical islands.

Inversion heaven, Pic dOrchy

Skirting the tops, Col d'Ourdayte

'You alright Jim? Did the most beautiful girl in Iraty keep you awake all last night?'

'Ha ha.'

'There's a hut below, we could stay there but we won't get to Lescun tomorrow if we do.'

'Nah, let's carry on.'

The path continues to contour across mountain faces of Otsogorritxipia, Otsogorrigagna and Chardekagagana (no... I haven't just dropped something on my keyboard) fairly effortlessly before one final steep climb to the last pass of the day Col d'Ourdayte. This has a real sting in its tail. I'm glad to reach its top. I spy Jim below, he seems to be looking up and shaking his fist, though I could have just made that up. Eventually he arrives and we high five because we're basically pricks at heart.

The path drops down into Spain, it's slow and loose underfoot, a shoulder of green grass juts out and below it, a stream bed makes the ideal place to spend the night.

Eight

Pitter patter pitter patter.

The rain is falling steadily and there's little wind to blow it away. It's time to dress in clothing designed to make walking as miserable and as hot as possible. The promise of happy dry walking in the rain has cost me many hundreds of pounds over the years. Different, all singing and dancing waterproofs have one thing in common. After a few hours in the wet I end up boiling hot, damp or wet inside and if I'm lucky, just gently streaming. To try and regulate my body temperature better I've taken to wearing a trekking skirt which basically lengthens your overpriced anorak to the knees. It means I don't overheat so quickly as when wearing waterproof trousers but I do look a bit of a fanny when it's on. So, suitably cloaked, it's time to move on.

We head down to the road and to the border crossing. In the distance the old refuge is a hive of activity. The builders are basically building a new one and using the old footprint as a template. It's great to see and we ponder if they'll finish in the next couple of hours so we can get a coffee. Unfortunately the roof isn't on yet so it looks unlikely. Passing here five years ago, the building was stripped bare. The windows, doors, the lead on the roof, infact, anything that could have been unscrewed had been nicked.

The beech forest is eerily quiet, the path weaves into the heart of this unspoiled wilderness as the rain pours down and the mud gloppy underfoot. The narrow track sends us deeper into this enchanted landscape. It could be a difficult place to navigate as the map contours look more like a bowl of spaghetti than hills. Luckily the avenue of trees is marked with odd splodges of paint and lead the way through to the twisted limestone plateau.

The rain eases after a few hours and bright patches of sky appear. The trees thin and the light grey cask landscape rolls out in front of us. Ribs of limestone score the valley side like piles of bones from the Jurassic era, shattered peaks tower above.

The valley floor has no river, water flows underground which probably explains why no one lives here. The final climb towards Col d'Anaye takes it out of me but at least I can now take off my mobile sauna as the sun is out. Jim's in front and looks quite pleased to see me suffering as we once more cross into France.

Sitting on a rock and marvelling at the view we see a woman in the distance with two dogs rounding up stray sheep on the hillside. After a bite to eat it's time to press on, we're still a long way from Lescun. Passing the shepherd, I say hello but she's not very friendly and says nothing and just stares. It's fairly obvious she resents us being there. We descend into a hanging valley, then drop steeply through trees, the track is cut into the cliff below, zig zagging down. More knee cartilage damage later and we arrive at Plateau de Sanchese, a 1000 metres below the pass two hours later. A long road walk to Lescun follows. As stunning as it is, I'm tired and the tarmac hurts. Arriving at the village we stock up on fresh food and head to the campsite. A new toilet block has been built since our last visit and with it, the price to camp has increased to pay for it. We go through the usual palaver of paying for two small tents that together take up less space than a barn size tent that most people bring, the owner isn't having it.

'You are in 2 tents. I charge for 2 tents and 2 people.'

We are pointed to the backpackers area which consists mainly of gravel and no shade, return trade from walkers cannot be a priority anymore. The campsite has an air of disorganisation, with pitches unnumbered I go and see if there's somewhere better.

'Jim, Up here!'

I find a nice flat spot of grass under a tree that they were probably saving for a motorhome.

'Oh well, it's their loss, we'll just stay an extra night and not pay them to make up the difference.'

'A fine idea Paul, shall we have a glass of wine to celebrate our arrival?'

The morning is spent eating pastries and drinking coffee. Odd bouts of lying down break up the monotony of boiling the kettle. The prime objective of a day off is to move as little as possible, in that respect the morning is a complete success. By 2pm, I've drank so much coffee I have the jitters and feel a bit sick. We've also eaten all the nice food so it's time to head back up to the village. The shops are shut until 4pm. We ponder what to do, remember, moving unnecessarily is not an option so go to the local bar. Being in France, it's all very pleasant. An afternoon sipping beer and people watching has inadvertently become today's main objective.

A Basset hound is being taken for a walk but stops just outside the bar and lies down, refusing to move. The owner tries coaxing it back into action but it's having none of it. She pulls and pushes it. It's not moving and probably weighs the same as a sack of spuds so there's no chance of picking it up. We watch on, this is gripping stuff, it's the sort of thing you could write a book about..The lady tuts loudly, says something in French that is probably very upsetting for a Basset hound and promptly disappears. The dog falls asleep, I get some more beers, we obviously can't leave yet, not without knowing the dog's fate. Half an hour later the lady returns and waggles a sausage in front of the dog's nose. It gets to its feet quickly, the sausage is pulled away. The owner is at last victorious pulling the dog around the corner.

Andy and John, whom I chatted to briefly before Iraty, walk past. I call them over, Andy has a large beer, John an ice cream. We waffle on talking HRP stuff. Andy demolishes his beer quickly and gets another, John has another ice cream.

'I'm sick of ice cream.'

'Have small beer,'

'Hmm, ok.'

John tells us he shouldn't really be drinking, he's on the

medication to stop blood clots in his brain, having recently fractured his skull

'Bloody hell, that sounds serious, you look so well.'

Andy comes back with beers and finishes the story.

'We were climbing at Baggy point. John was leading and fell ten metres, the protection pulled out as he dropped and he landed on his head!'

'Yeah, I split open my skull, fractured my wrist too.' That healed quickly, I was lucky. I've been told to do nothing strenuous for three months until the swelling in my brain has gone down.'

'When was this?'

'Four weeks ago, I shouldn't really be here but I got bored, we planned this trip ages ago.'

'So you're carrying a twenty kilo pack over the Pyrenees and have been told not to do anything strenuous..'

'Yeah well, it's not so hard.'

I look at my watch and it's six pm, if we don't get to the shop soon they'll sell all the nice bread. We sit and ponder, beer or bread? The shop wins and I bag the last of the baguettes. Back to the tent and the evening is then spent fine dining.

❄ ❄ ❄

INTO THE FRENCH NATIONAL PARK

Col d'Anaye

Nine

'Ready?'
'Ready!'

We walk out of the campsite and up the road, it's always a good start to the day when you've just saved twenty two euros. A network of quiet country lanes is followed for the next hour. Once off the road we climb steadily and enter the Parc National, now at the start of what's considered the true Pyrenees. I celebrate by making a coffee, neither of us have much energy today after yesterday's hardships so sit idly dangling our feet in the stream.

Pushing on uphill a cabane is passed and outside six pigs lay side by side in the mud like an enormous pack of sausages. Eventually Col du Pau is reached and we're back at around the 2000 metre mark. A family is walking with a donkey carrying their camping gear. The donkey is standing eating grass, kids are sitting on the path and both parents are waving their arms and shouting whatever French is for 'giddy up'. The donkey is happy in the knowledge he can do what he likes because if you don't like it, you can carry your own crap. In the distance Pic Rouge stands out against the bright blue sky. It is indeed bright red. The path winds it way high along the ridge line, I see a suitable rock and grab a pew.

I look up at a group of hikers who are coming from the opposite direction.

'Are you OK? Have you cut yourself?'

'No, I'm fine. Just looking at the view, it's quite a climb up.'

'Oh I see, you've come from Lescun, there's splodges of blood all along the path, we thought it was you.'

Jim and I look at each other.

'Maybe John's brain is trying to pop out of his nose?'

'Should have stuck to the ice cream I guess.'

Later on the track there's dark blobs here and there, they continue for a hundred metres or so, then stop. It could be blood or could be wine, it's difficult to tell, especially for Jim as both flow through him in equal measures.

The track skirts below Pic Rouge. The rock seems to be molten and pink but in it are round white pebbles. It looks like the big bars of nougat that were sold next to candy floss at funfairs, the stuff you only buy once because A. It's disgusting and B. It'll pull your teeth out when you bite into it.

A short drop to a grassy plateau and then it's up to Lac d'Arlet. We walk over to the refuge and sit in the sun. Andy and John are nowhere to be seen. If it was John earlier, he must be alright now as they have carried on.

We put up our tents and a few hours later, a family appear just before dark with a donkey trailing behind.

Donkey business

Pic Rouge

Ten

The sun warms the tent as it breaks over the horizon at six am, by seven, it's too hot to stay inside so we lazily make breakfast sitting on the shore. I jump in the lake for a swim and make a vow to jump in one every day, as long as the sun's out that is. Sitting and letting the warm rays dry me, I watch two kids running around after a donkey. Once caught, they smack its rump, the donkey moves quickly to where they are camped. I hope the parents are taking note.

It's an easy climb to start from the lake to a low pass, mountain silhouettes fan out and fill the skyline, through a gap the distinctive mitten shape of Pic du Midi is seen rising supreme. The day's a hot one but quick progress is made following a steady highline below the top of PIc d'Arri to the end of a jutting out ridge at 1909 metres. With fine views back to pic d'Anie and across to Pena Colorada, we take an early break. From here there's nowhere else to go but down for 800 metres. At the river we make a detour and head down a long road walk to Forges d'Abel, a village notable for nothing notable to say about it.

The gravel layby is hot, the road dead, I try my luck hitching but can't really be bothered as a bus is due in ten minutes, so give up. It feels strange to be in a vehicle as it winds its way down through the mountains. The valley narrows to a gorge passing under Fort du Portalet, a fortification built into the cliff that took nearly thirty years to complete. The valley bottom opens to a wide flat plain, hills spread out either side with the village of Bedous at the far end.

As it's too early to camp, we decide to go and have a look around. It's a Sunday and Bedous is deadly quiet, I'm expecting a gunfight at any minute. A quick tour offers no Alimentation or Newsagent. A supermarket recently built in the next village has put pay to that. There is a bakery but it's closed today. Rounding a street corner a sleeping dog jumps to its feet when it see's us and starts growling and barking. At first I'm nice to it, I like dogs and I like to think they like me. This one though is getting really angry, I change my opinion and like all dogs but this one and try to kick it as it gets closer to take a bite. It then goes batshit at me so I stop and take off my pack. Pulling out a walking pole, I am now ready to skewer the fucker like a vietnamese kabab. The dog sees the pole and slinks off growling.

On the next street, we see a man smoking outside a bar, he's a cheery sort, so head inside. Maurice has owned the bar for four years, it's as laid back in there as he is. Mellow music is playing. We pull up two stools and order a Belgian beer. A dog walks in and sits by my feet, it's the same one that just tried biting me, I stroke its ears tentatively at first thinking it's just a ploy to bite my hand off.

'So Maurice, you send your dog out to scare tourists shitless so they hide in here. Very cunning.'

'But of course, I need your money!'

Maurice used to travel the world as a cheese connoisseur. At private parties he would be asked to present the best cheese to go with certain wines. The cheese should never overpower the wine and vice versa. I look at him in disbelief when he tells us of being flown to Hollywood and then to Cannes with a suitcase I'm guessing, full of Red Leicester and Dairy Lea? He also tells us of the massive storms that can build up at Bedous. Being nestled in the foothills, the heat off the plains collides with the mountains and Bedous being in the middle bears the brunt of it. Hail, the size of golfballs, have smashed the roofs in the village to pieces, so much so, they are now tiled with small slates to make repair easier.

Taking in all this knowledge has made me thirsty so we order more beer, after all, it's only four in the afternoon and what else is there to do? Some locals come in, we chat and I realise that I've had no lunch but nothing really matters anymore. More dog tickling ensues, Maurice brings out some cheese and crackers, oh well, best have another beer then.

I feel very pissed. 'How strong is this beer?'

'6.8%'

'Ahh, jolly good that explains it. Two more please.'

'OK, If you buy one more I will buy you one back.'

And so it goes. Everyone in the bar is my best friend, we feel like hero's returning from a great adventure. At some point we are fed meat. I'm so drunk by now, moving off the stool seems an impossible task so order another beer instead. It's also become dark ouside. How did that happen?

I turn to Jim. 'I have to go now or I'll fall asleep in the toilet.'

'Sounds good, I've just tried making a cigarette for ten minutes and failed miserably.'

I muster all my mental strength and stand up.

'Right.'

Victorious, we now swing on our packs then hug and wish everyone a 'bonne nuit'

'Go down the road and over the railway line, there's a picnic area by the river.' Maurice tells us as we wobble into the night.

Nylon gently brushes my cheek, hmm... Where am I? And why have I got trainers on inside my sleeping bag? I open my eyes, the tent is draped over me like the Turin Shroud. Crawling out I see our surroundings for the first time. We are camped on some gravel next to a railway track, twenty metres away is a perfect stretch of grass with the picnic table next to the river. So close but yet so far.. Taking down the tents is easy as only two pegs actually stayed in. We saunter into town, get some pastries and go for a coffee. The village has a Camping Municipal. These are my favourite campsites, built sometime in the nineteen sixties, they have all you need, hot and cold water that normally takes turns to come out the shower, nice flat shady pitches and above all, cheap.

The supermarket is three miles away along a pencil straight road so we hitch there and back. I'm getting journey updates from Jason, a friend who's joining us. So far, a tube to my uncle's to drop off his belongings, another across London, the Gatwick express, a plane to Lourdes, a taxi, a train to Pau and now another train to Bedous.

I go to the station to meet him and there he is, my best mate for thirty years.

'Well done.'

'I feel cheated Paul, surely you could have got a boat in there somewhere.'

The three of us head to last night's bar for a beer. A middle aged hippy couple are dancing, the man is grinning hysterically, It looks like they've just got together and he can't believe his luck. Others are smoking cigarettes whilst sitting on bar stools, all it would take is a young Gerard Depardieu to walk in wearing denim flares to complete the scene.

Maurice welcomes us like lost brothers. He fills us in on some missing details.

'You were fine until you got to eight pints.. After that you became hopeless.'

Eleven

The morning starts with a hitch to the supermarket and we stock up for the next six days. I take Jason to the blandest shelves having dragged him away from all the lovely fresh produce, it being too heavy. The basket is filled with packet soups, couscous, cheese, chocolate, nuts, muesli, bread.

'This is what you need.'

'Nice..and parole is when exactly?'

We gorge on fruit and fresh bread whilst watching a paraglider float down. A tourist is strapped to his chest and yelping with delight having made it to terrafirma and not broken a leg. It's a ninety minute wait for the bus back up the valley, so an afternoon start. Like magic the bus appears, none of us being overly confident this would happen as the bus timetable had so many amendments attached, it would even confuse Alan Turing. The driver tells us the bus only goes up to Col du Somport on the weekend so we have to get off at Forges d'Abel. It's annoying but at least mine and Jim's journey remains unbroken.

Trudging up the road, there's little traffic as a tunnel takes most of it to Spain these days. It's very hot so we weave an erratic course aiming for whichever side the trees offer shade from the midday sun. After twenty minutes a bus is coming down the hill. It's our bus, the driver waves, we wave back confused and then realise.

'Bloody hell! We could have stayed on the bus through the tunnel to Spain and then over the pass back to France.'

'Why did he tell us to get off? The prick!'

Walking on, it is boring but the miles have to be done, music makes the next hour tolerable. A Compostela route has been running parallel with the road but frustratingly can't be reached until now. It follows the river and offers shade and rejoins the road near the top. A bus comes towards us, it's our bus again! He's done another lap in the two hours it's taken us to walk to the top of the pass. He waves, I look at him and give him a flick of the V's.

A quick hop into Spain and a cafe looks very inviting. We all want a beer but there's still a long way to go so sit with cokes and try to look happy as the cokes cost more than the beers that everyone else it is drinking. The defunct ski town of Astun is our next port of call, the road to it could be described as a plod at best. Astun itself is an Eighties horror show of crap architecture, everything is boarded up and shut. At least the roads are over now, a path lazily follows a stream upwards, when the ski town disappears out of sight there is a feeling of relief as we eventually arrive at Ibon de Ascalar, a small lake hidden from the rubbish below. I stick my hand in, it's as warm as bath water. The sun is low but if I get in now it'll be bliss. Attempts at swimming are none too successful alas, as the lake is very shallow. I stand in the middle of the lake waist deep. Unfortunately from the knees down I'm in mud.

We bang up the tents, it's nearly dark already. I promise Jason there's better to come but I think he's too tired to care or to bother thinking about it as he forces down packet pea soup.

Hospice

The oxygen gently hisses, rasping breaths cause my mums chest to gently shake as it rises up and down.

'What's happened?' I look at my sister.

'She was OK this morning, we ate strawberries and then....'

I don't remember what else was said. I turn away, my emotions are so numb now I've become disconnected with the reality I'm facing. I watch the Ox eye daisies sway in a gentle summer breeze though open patio doors that lead to decking outside. Gardens spill seamlessly into the Herefordian landscape. The hospice has a calming finality.

After a couple of hours, I kiss and say goodbye, even now I mutter, I'll see you tomorrow. Brown eyes flicker open, the heavy sedation cannot stop the only part of my mother's body that can still move. We look deeply at each other for a couple of seconds, and then they shut. A million words could not express a better farewell.

Amanda goes back to the hospice later just to check on things. At six am I awake with a start, for an hour I then doze, I hear the front door open, footsteps on the stairs and the bedroom door opens.

'She's gone Paul.'

Twelve

The path cuts up the green bowl above and heads up to Col des Moines and back into France. The shite of yesterday couldn't seem further away, lakes and crumpled ridges fill the scene, an inversion gently bubbles far below, snaking its way into the lowlands.

Above it all Pic du Midi stands supreme, taking centre stage.

'There we are Jay, that's better isn't it?'

We drop down to Lac Casterau and then further into the valley as the mist burns off above the river. A cabane is reached, sheep are milling around and bleating, shiney pots and urns are neatly stacked by the cabanes doorway, a lad of around eleven years old jumps up onto his feet when he sees us.

'You want my cheese?'

'Maybe, what's it like?'

Three of the thinnest slivers it's possible to cut with a knife are brought out, he's been taught well. It dissolves on the tongue, there's no need to chew.

We don't really need it as our packs already have a brick each of the stuff inside but order three 300 gram lumps anyway and part with nine euros. I watch him through the doorway as he cuts it, smiling. He comes back out and hands us three little cheese triangles and then runs inside, I can hear him proudly telling his story to someone.

A grassy gully behind the cabane heralds the start of a long climb, it enters a small hidden glen, purple irises spread up its sides. Looking back, the serrated ridge line of the Spanish border adds to the remoteness, I marvel at the scene, Jim appears and digs out his food bag.

'Shall we have lunch and try our new cheese?'

Ten minutes later Jason comes around the corner, dumps his rucksack and sits next to me.

'Shit, I've really let myself go, I'm knackered.'

'Too many pasties lad? you've obviously been enjoying yourself this summer.'

I was a little surprised when I saw him get off the train at Bedous. A runner who normally looks after himself, Jason had the appearance of someone who couldn't say no when offered an extra slice of cake. In fact, I've never seen him so big in thirty years. We try and get together once a year as he now lives in New York. This normally involves a remote campsite, bimbles up a hill and then beers whilst sitting in a car listening to music like degenerates from Wayne's World. With the house sold and a hastily arranged Pyrenean trip thrown into the mix, he gives the impression of some who's been duped. This was after all, supposed to be a holiday for him.

'It'll get easier, normally after five or six days..'

'I'm only here for the week!'

We carry on up to Lac de Petreget nestled under Pic du Midi's steep sided flanks and jump in the lake washing off the day's toils. Its shallows are warm but the deeper waters have a bite. We float looking up at the jumble of rock towering up to the mountain's summit. One final push and it's a long flat track to the other side of Midi and the busy Refuge de Pombie.

Refuges attract a variety of people, families, walking groups, all well behaved and normally in bed by nine pm. I was sitting outside of one years ago and could hear a woman describing the view in detail behind me. I looked around and she was sitting with her husband who had gone blind, he listened intently with a smile on his face. I looked back across to the view as she carried on talking, it was deeply touching.

Pic du Midi d'Ossau

Thirteen

'Where are we heading today chief?'

'The other side of those hills, it's quite a long day..'

Jim looks across at me but says nothing. He hasn't smoked much this morning, he's not stupid.

Across the valley is a string of 3000 metre high peaks with Balaitus at 3148metres taking prime position. They look and are, miles away. Firstly we have to drop 700 metres to the road, then head back up to Col d'Arrious and Col d'Arremoulit and into Spain, it's another three hours to Refugio de Respomuso to finish . I choose not to mention any of this to Jason because I hate to see a grown man cry.

It starts well, dropping quite quickly down to the road past high pastures and through a beech forest. We stop for a break just before the road, there's a large lay by but alas, no snack van.

'OK I'm putting on some music, see you in an album or two.'

'Good idea, we'll be at the top then. Yeah?'

'We'll be somewhere up there.' And point at nothing in particular.

I head off, having been up this way twice before, I feel bad as I know this is going to hurt. Up through trees a bridge crosses the stream. As is becoming customary I take off my sweat soaked shirt and chuck it in, once back on it's instantly cooling. Back to it, a series of endless zig zags is then tackled until we reach a cabane. It's been built using a massive boulder for one wall which must offer protection against avalanches. Or maybe they had just run out of stone so used one big one instead. It's also an album of music later, so time for a break.

Jim and I sit munching lunch as Jason does the last zag.

'I'm really annoyed with myself, fuck I'm unfit.'

'Your doing good.'

'How much further is it to the top?'

'We're about half way.'

'Your joking right?.. Oh shit.'

The climb continues, looking back, Pic du Midi has a big mushroom cloud sat on its top. The enclosed nature of the valley makes it feel claustrophobic, there seems little air with the sun beating down. I push on to the top of the pass watching sweat drip off my nose as I do so. Ten minutes later Jason appears, he's smiling.

'Well done, you've got to the top.. Of this bit . You are OK with heights aren't you?'

The Passage d'Orteig cuts across the mountainside. A steel cable is placed along it to help steady any nerves. It looks a lot worse than it is and we soon cross it. A land of rock lies ahead. Glaciers have smoothed the granite into gentle bluffs of which a path snakes its way across. It's a stark and foreboding place, it's also about half way as Refuge d'Areemouit is reached. We sit and look at the view. Out of all the refuges past on this walk this one has to be the least appealing, small and dark, a large tent is attached to it for extra bunk space. In my three visits, the sky has always been cold and grey, matching the landscape in a seamless blanket devoid of colour. Once across to the other side of the lake, talus litters the high cirque, we pick a line through it and some boulder hopping later, we are at Col d'Arre Moulit and back on the Spanish border. Standing on a cliff-like edge, a lake shines teasingly below.

Col d'Arre Moulit

'This is very steep, try not to fall off will you'

'Thanks Paul, that's very helpful'

It's a clamber down at best, Pic Palas is at the head of the cirque, Balaitous to the right, cliffs line Lac d'Arriels shore. Through it all our route treads a course to another boulder field and then to the first lake. I stand and wince watching my compatriots hopping over the loose rocks. A broken leg here would be very bad news. The next smaller lake is half empty, a new dam has been built but still needs the winter's snow to fill it. We intersect a valley high up on its flank. In the distance is a dam and behind it is the highest pub in the Pyrenees. It takes forever to reach the dam following an old water duct from the two lakes earlier. Its concrete top has collapsed in places, the hydro scheme here has definitely seen better days. I can almost taste the beer but it's just out of reach, a short rise then gives everyone a sense of humour failure before Refugio de Respomuso comes into view.

We sit outside, pints in hand whilst the refuge hums full to the brim of Spanish enjoying their three course meal. A cold wind blows continually, funneling across the lake at 2200mtrs as the sun starts to set, turning the peaks to the east golden.

'See that peak on the right hand side?'

'The one that looks like a shark's fin?'

'Yep. We're going up that tomorrow'

There's a silence as a wave of tiredness hits, Jim finishes his cigarette.

'We best get one more round in, it's going to be dark in half an hour'

Fourteen

I'm crumpled at the bottom of the tent. Not for the first time, I have to haul myself back up as every turn means a slide of six inches down, I've drawn the short straw and get the grassy incline. All three tents are wedged in a small grassy ravine ten minutes walk up the track from the Refugio. Once back on the trail and past the massive reservoir, the valley floor opens up to a grassy meadow that's pancake flat, it feels as remote a spot as you're ever likely to reach. Grande Fashe, our peak for the day looks daunting. Other 3000 metre peaks jostle in the skyline. A half finished dam is at one end, its crumbling concrete walls abandoned, a lucky escape for this beautiful valley. We pass a small natural lake, the water's freezing but I need to freshen up, Jason jumps in too, I think he might even be starting to enjoy himself. Jim sits on the bank smoking a fag.

At the end of the meadow, the valley squeezes in close. Following a stream the grassy slopes are once more replaced with rock. A track cuts a ledge across the scree high above a small lac before the final pull to the top of the pass. Col de Cache 2664 metres.

Grande Fache towers intimidatingly above, cloud scuds across its summit. I feel uneasy about going up as we start picking our way through its shattered slopes, it soons steepens to a scramble, the rock is really loose and is flaking badly. We take it in turns climbing sections of it and spread out in case of rockfall. Jim goes ahead and around the side of a chimney of sorts, Jason and I hear a weird yelping noise as a water bottle bounces past us.

'It's not this way', he shouts.

'I can see that'

We edge further up, although only 350 metres above the Col, it seems to be taking forever. A couple of pinnacles are traversed and then another scramble to its top at 3005 metres.

'Woooo hoooo!'

Jason pondering the cost of helicopter evacuation - Grande Fashe

Going back down is easier, another route is chosen and although just as shitty underfoot, we descend quickly and are soon back to the packs. I can see the Refuge Wallon way below from the col, it looks about the same size as a Monopoly board hotel from here, a tiny cube of civilization. For the next two hours we head slowly down, the path is well made but full of rounded rocks like golf balls, it makes for a frustratingly slow descent doing a massive zig zag to ease the angle. Jim and I are well ahead, we have walking poles and years of grinding out days like this behind us, eventually the valley floor is reached. We sit and wait..

Jason collapses beside us with all the grace of someone who's just been shot.

Jim looks at me. 'Paul, I think it's time to put him out of his misery.'

'Well, there's two options. The first one is to continue over two high passes to Viganamale. There's a refuge below its impressive north face where we can camp and sup wine on the refuge's balcony for the evening, then walk out to Cauterets the next day.' 'Or... We can head out tomorrow, get to Cauterets in the afternoon, have a pizza and some beers, then spend all day Saturday watching football as it's the first day of the season.'

'Hmm, I need to think about this one.'

We get to Wallon at five pm. There's a lot of tents up already which is a surprise. On our last visit here I remember a park warden marching around at six pm fining campers, he stomps over to my recently erected tent looking flustered with rage before going into a French monologue I don't understand.

'Could you say that again in English please?' I say with a slight grin.

This obviously makes him turn a bit purple as he repeats it. 'You can not bivouac before seven pm, it is forbidden!'

I reply, a lie so feeble I wonder why I start to say it, 'I'm just drying out my tent, it got quite damp this morning you see..'

'I don't care if you have been soaking wet all day and have hypothermia! Take down zat tent!'

Anyway, he's not about, probably got another job more fulfilling like torturing spies or something, we put up our tents and head to the refuge.

At the refuge they are having a little sing along, taking it in turns to play. Some are better than others but the bar has been set pretty low to start with and it's quite painful to listen to so we head back to the tents with some wine. The sky has been darkening for the last hour and the air is still and hot, there's a boom of thunder and the heavens open so we duck into our tents. After a few minutes I can hear heavy breathing and chewing, I look out and a dozen cows are scattered around us. One shoots out a liquid shit missile that narrowly avoids my tent, they seem quite oblivious to us, so all thoughts of being trampled by half a ton of bovine fade away and I lie back down.

A Royal Wedding

The cardboard tray is buckling under the weight of three large cappuccinos. The corridors have become so familiar, a snaking route through the new hospital to a glass lined passageway to the prefabs at the back. They were supposed to be knocked down but bad planning means the beds were still needed. The ward has an ingrained faint smell, at first you can't make it out, then it comes to you, vomit and shit.

At the far end past beds of people in various states of decay are two ladies chatting away watching TV, as I get closer, my Mother looks up.

'Ah my boy, there you are, just in time, she's come out.'

'I was hoping it would be over by the time I got back.'

'Don't be so miserable.'

I pass over the coffees and grab a plastic chair. Megan walks out of the front door over to the carriage. It's Royal Wedding day and the hospital, in an unbelievable act of generosity, has put it on the TV for free.

'Oh isn't she lovely, look at that dress!'

'Oh yes look at her... This coffee is delicious, thank you.' Geraldine exclaims.

Mum and her new friend Geraldine have been watching for an hour, they both have the same yellow pallor and bag of piss hanging off their beds. Having been in the ward for over two weeks, my Mother is not surprisingly, at her wits end. The stents in her liver have blocked and the cysts that are growing on it have been drained. A course of bad arse antibiotics are trying to clear an ongoing infection so we can go home. There's talk of it being tomorrow. For this moment in time, she's happy and for that, I thank you Harry and Megan.

Marcadau Valley

Fifteen

It's a well worn track from Wallon down to Pont d Espagne. The river's lively, cutting its way though the mountains blanketed with ancient pines, they give welcome shade as we pass families picnicking in the many grassy meadows. At the road head we have lunch, forcing down stale bread and ripe cheese. If I don't eat it now it'll be binned in a few hours. Sipping some wine that was left over from last night, I take in my surroundings. Pont d'Espagne is full of tourists up for the day, apart from an impressive waterfall, there's little to do for the less energetic types other than eat ice cream and mill about. I feel self conscious as they walk past smelling of soap in their white socks and sandals. I have sandals on too but my feet are black with dust and I smell of ground in sweat. We look like mountain tinkers. We are mountain tinkers.

I wasn't really looking forward to today but it's turning out to be a delight. The river drops steeply into a series of cataracts and waterfalls, the path sticks close and is shaded, it's also smooth and well graded so we zip down at a pace. A hot springs hotel fills the valley floor, tourist shops with whistling marmots and picture plate coasters line the roadside. The restaurants look very inviting but we soldier on for another half an hour and arrive in the centre of Cauterets. Jason and I sit and watch the world go about its business as Jim looks for the cheapest bar. It feels like we've just landed in a spaceship as it's the first busy town for nearly three weeks. Jim does well as the bar even sells pizza.

The sky is thick with fog as it gently drizzles, big umbrellas offer protection as pain au raisins and almond croissants are eaten with coffee so strong it could wake the dead, the perfect accompaniment. The cafe owner struts around wearing a kilt, he's an ex rugby player, what he lacks in finesse, he makes up for in bringing another coffee with just a wave of the finger. We were actually only asking for the bill but thought it best not to argue.

We do a tour of Cauterets most promising streets and a likely looking bar is found. The owner searches the networks, he knows there's money to be made if he finds the right game. Flicking through the channels and there it is. Arsenal versus Newcastle. Success!

Arsenal even win.. It's a miracle! With nothing else pressing, we then sit and watch Chelsea versus... who gives a shit. It's a day of much hilarity, there's a lot to be said for life long friendships. I apologise for the torture Jason has just had to endure, he pretends he actually enjoyed the challenge. With that, I know he must be drunk so we continue drinking into the evening and talking complete bollocks.

As Stephen Hawking once said. 'It's the past that tells us who we are. Without it we lose our identity.'

Jason packs. He's been using all my cast-offs because when he flew to the UK six weeks ago, we hadn't planned any of this. My thermarest has a puncture so I swap it for my old yellow one he's been using, it's bitter sweet, even though it stays up, it's three quarter length and narrow so it's like trying to sleep on an inflated scaffold plank. We also get shot of some maps. I have a dig through my stuff and give him my unused water filter.

Jim and I had planned to walk in the afternoon but it's still raining so we see Jason off on the bus and then go to the shop.

'What's that Paul?'

'A stick of deodorant.'

'So you send back a water filter which could be very useful and replace it with some deodorant?'

'Of course! I've let myself go for far too long on this trip.'

* * *

OFF ROUTE AND AROUND ODESA

Above canon de Aniclo

Sixteen

We drag ourselves away from the comforts of the campsite and Cauterets, the longer you leave it the harder it gets. For the next five days we'll be on our own, no guide book to lead the way as we plan to wander spectacularly off route.

The sky is oppressive and as thick and white as gloss paint, it deadens the air. We need to head due south to get back to the high Pyrenees, so follow the valle de Lutour and its lively river. With a series of waterfalls and deep pools, it has become a picnicker's heaven. Alas it's cold and miserable today, the steady stream of day trippers keep walking unsure of what to do next. After three hours we arrive at Lac d'Estom, walkers drift in and out of view in the damp mist, having gone uphill for 900 metres they look none too pleased. An Alpine scene fills the head of the valley but all that can be seen today is a thick pea souper. We hunker down and have lunch. Once away from the refuge, the GR we've been following runs out and turns into a route. Picking our way up through slimy rock we traverse high above the lac and lose the path, voices are heard above so we head their way across scree as the faint shadows of walkers come into view. They talk of an inversion high up and the camping is 'Tres jolie!'

Lac d'Labas drifts in and out of thick cloud, we've now gone uphill 1500 metres but still seen nothing so press on to Lac de Oulettes. Upon arrival, a curtain of light, a patch of blue above and the world once more turns technicolor, fog swirls in waves over the lac's surface.

'Woow. Look at that!' A circle of high cliffs appears like Kong Island out of the mist.

'This'll do nicely.'

Jim drops his rucksack on a perfect patch of flat grass.We sit in sunshine and make a brew watching the inversion bubble up and down just below us.

Lac de Oulettes

Seventeen

The day starts bright. It looks on the map a fairly easy one but high mountains normally have other ideas that put pay to that. A narrow path threads its way up to Lac Couy, it's a labyrinth of high lakes, peaks and hidden cwm's. An area of high pasture with rock formations folded and striped, leads to high corrie filled with rock and scree. The ridge line above is black and cut like the teeth of a saw. I spot a flash of red and see a climber high on Peak d'Estom as we reach Col des Gentaines at 2729 metres.

Ahead is Vignemale, its glacier receding leaving polished slopes. Above, bands of rock glow grey, red and orange and the sky is as blue as listerine mouthwash.

'My phone says there's a path over there just below Peak Mourou.

It must be a viewpoint shall we go over and see?'

Jim looks across and I can tell he's searching for a reason not too.

'Come on, we'll be able to see Gavarnie and such like, maybe even a donkey or two."

The view is as good as any peak. We are after all, at 2800 metres. Out to the east, the mass of Cirque Gavarnie, Le Tallon and Breche Roland. Back to the west is a jumble of peaks that we've already passed, right in the distance we can make out pic d' Anie, the first high mountain peak encountered eleven days ago. It already feels like I've been doing this forever, I guess I have, with odd bouts of work to fund it. The route down picks its way through bluffs and drops 500 metres to the GR10.

'We should do more stuff like that, get off route and have a poke around the high places, take a load of food up to a high camp'

'That's next year sorted then'

With the GR10 comes a well worn path that's easy to follow once more and with it we drop another 700 metres to Barrage d'Ossoue, a small dammed lake. A brief swim and a second lunch is consumed. Whilst drying off, I look back up at the wall of mountains craning my neck, a small notch sits in the ridge line, our viewpoint, I marvel at it

'Hey Jim, that's where we were four hours ago.'

'No wonder my knees are bolloxed.'

Heading towards Gavarnie the sun angles low. Our route sticks to the hillside following the GR10 for the next hour until we branch off right and past Cabane Sausse. A large herd of cows look on, there's little water so instead of going further up, we opt to camp in the valley.

The King Of Vignemale

Count Henry Russell, or 'The King of Vignemale' as he was known to his friends, had climbed Vignemale thirty three times. He was quite plainly bonkers about Vignermale and not being content with the numerous ascents, in 1888 requested to lease the mountain for 99 years for one franc a year. 'Just the glacier, snow and rocks and summit.' He had no interest in the land below.

He noted. 'It is certainly the highest property in Europe'. ' One adopts a mountain, one marries it, one presents it proudly to one's friends, one has eyes for nothing else. That is what happened to me with Vignemale. Because of living there I fell in love with it.'

One of his first jobs on his new proposition was to build a two metre high cairn, as Vignemale stood at 2998 metres so making it 3000 metres. These things being very important to a tidy and ordered person.

To make access easier, Russelll became the instigator of the mountain hut system in the surrounding area. He was spurred on by nearly dying on Breche de Roland some years earlier. Having tried and abandoned climbing a peak above Gavarnie, he returned quickly to the Breche de Roland in the evening trying to escape an approaching storm. He was too late and got caught in it, spending the night on the Breche under falling snow he took to running on the spot in an attempt not to die of cold. He returned to Gavarnie in the morning where they thought his appearance was like a ghost as he was thought to be dead.

He also invented, or popularised, the mountain sleeping bag used by a few shepherds before he had a taste for spending nights on the summits of mountains. So he carried a bag made of the skin of six sheep!

Sometimes this quite plainly wasn't enough so he asked his guides to bury him in blankets and stone on the summit of Vignemale with just his head poking out spending the night there. He wanted to 'feel the mountain, to be the mountain'. Whilst his guides froze solid through the night, Russell stood cocooned until 4am in the morning, extracting himself and telling all what a success it was.

This gave him the flavour to spend more nights on top so set about building caves to sleep in. The rock was as hard as granite despite being limestone so progress was slow as tools kept on breaking. A blacksmith suggested bringing up a mini forge to repair tools up there. This saved time and the first cave finished, complete with an iron door, it was named 'Villa Russell.' He then had the cave baptised by a local priest. Another two caves were made later. One for guests and one for ladies. Dynamite had recently been discovered so this made the job a whole lot easier.

Guests came often. One particular large banquet has become legend. Fifteen guests plus porters filled up the mountain and stayed for three nights. A tent was erected outside the three caves and they dined in comfort. Equipped with rugs, armchairs and bedding, Eskimo costumes, oriental perfumes and lanterns. This was supplemented by fine cigars, wine and a leg of ham so large that it could have served as a cushion. Russell would dress in his finest city clothes, serve warm wine and take them to the top of Pique Longue to watch the sunset.

'These quiet Pyrenees are made to be my mountains.' He once said.

I couldn't agree more.

Vignemale

Eighteen

A steep climb first thing leads to a grassy bowl. There's no path, we are following a red line indicated on a free map app on my phone which is not marked at all on our paper map. We have no idea if the route we are following is a walk, a scramble or worse. I've noticed a lot of these happy little red lines can take you anywhere you like. Like the top of Vignemale for instance.

A grassy ramp leads to the main ridge. Cloud bubbles just below, it's inversion heaven once more. I look up at the ridge, it's narrow but fine, the little red line today will not necessitate a change of underwear. The top of Pic De Saint Andre 2608 metres soon follows, views abound in all directions. This peak is ours for the day, I feel very smug having escaped the crowds, albeit briefly. We drop back down into fog and then head up to Pic entre Les Ports. Bizarrely the inversion stops bang on the border, a pylon stands like a sentinel against it. 'Sorry we don't want your sort in Spain, move back please'

Swallows mow the hillside for insects, there must be close to a hundred, swooping low, back and forth. Walkers mill just below, a high road to Pic de Tentes is a handy stop off point for those wanting to go up to Breche de Roland, a spectacular cliff with a notch in the middle which you can cross through to Spain which is our next objective. A constant stream of people seem to be heading both ways, the path blazes a way through barren rock contouring around the mountainside before pulling up to Refuge Sarradets which is perched just below the Breche. There's no water and the refuge is shut for renovations as it was originally built in 1956. A new extension has been built out of Corten steel and complements the scene. I'm not into new architecture but this works. Well done to whoever.

Spanish border patrol

I'm out of water so I walk over to the last of last winter's snow and gather some melt water to drink. It's gritty but it will do, a water filter would have been handy..There's no snow bank below the Breche, it looks odd without it and it leaves a powdery scree slope instead, a moving conveyor belt, two steps up, one slide down. It's a pull to the top and we've hit the rush hour of people coming down, flicking gravel all over the place. I sit in the notch of one of the most spectacular mountain scenes in the world. Just me, one hundred Germans and Jim.

Breche de Roland, doing a fine impression of Noahs Ark

I came through here the first time fifteen years ago, a chain was bolted high up the cirque above Spain, it was quite terrifying. Following a group along it, the chain was clammy from all the sweaty palms before me, the drop below massive. For some reason I reflect about the experience to Jim.

'Shall we do that then?'

'Err well, it also ends in a massive boulder field, it's not a nice route.'

'I like the sound of that, let's do it shall we?'

'Err, Well.. Err, bollox. Okay then.'

A narrow ledge cuts across the bottom of a cliff and then the chain appears, I'm fifteen years older now and full of dread, not knowing how bad it would be last time also helped. Although bolted at ten metre intervals, the chain has an alarming habit of swinging outwards as you hold on. To make matters more interesting the ledge now disappears to some rocky stumps or just a plain rock face, nicely polished at an angle to pad against. All of this with a mere drop of around 200 metres below. Just when you think it won't get any worse an overhang appears, I crouch as low as possible but get my walking poles jammed on the overhang above. They are tied to my pack and I'm wedged solid, I can't go backwards either.

'You'll have to swing out on the chain.' Jim helpfully suggests.

'What!'

'Push your feet on the rock, lean back and stick your arse out into oblivion whilst holding onto the chain and pull yourself around.'

'Are you fucking mad.!!'

I wiggle and drop to a knee, I'm now kind of crawling/hauling myself along using the chain across the sloping rock face and squeeze through and around the corner.

'Jesus..Okay your turn.'

I stand eagerly awaiting Jim's shrieks but he goes underneath with no bother and unscathed.

'No problem.'

'Yeah well, I guess being the size of a hobbit comes in handy sometimes.'

We pick our way through the boulders, some are the size of cars, it's slow going as the rocks wobble alarmingly. A family is in front, teenage boys are scouting the area for a way out and the father looks like a man who has just been given an earful. The wife sees us approach and pleads.

'Do you know the way?'

'It's over there I think, I'll go and have a look, wait here.'

I follow a ledge, it's then a simple climb up a small rock face to another ledge and easier ground.

'From here the rest is easy, that is not too bad.' I shout pointing at the drop below.

'We go this way.' The wife shouts back, pointing to a series of never ending bluffs to the valley floor.

A few minutes later Jim appears.

'She was having none of it, that chain finished her off earlier.'

Once around the corner, a long grassy bowl stretches underneath, the small hills that undulate on the other side look like they have been cast from a jelly mold. It's high, arid country, a real Sierra landscape. Our track stays high and level joining another from the valley below so we keep up a good pace, unfortunately stream beds are dry, what water there is has disappeared underground through the limestone. The place we want to camp at only has a stagnant pool for water so we begrudgingly push on to the Goriz hut, infamous for its overcrowding. The Spanish forbid camping in the park but allow it at the hut, so anyone who comes to Ordesa, which is one of Spain's most popular national parks, and wants to go backpacking, will end up here, just like us.

As we get closer a scene reminiscent of a mini music festival unfolds, tents are dotted on every flat or slightly sloping piece of ground, well over fifty of them. More people keep arriving at the same time as us, I look at it in disbelief. We are all looking for the same thing- to be out in the wilds, none of us have found it today unfortunately. I get a couple of small beers from the refuge and we sit in the last of the evening sun. We are just happy to chill and people watch. Good job too, there's plenty here.

A couple arrive, they are young and very excited. It looks like it's the first time they've camped more than two metres away from a car. Once the tent is up they start photographing themselves at every single angle possible, with tent and without. The girl is a selfie expert and not content with the results, starts doing handstands whilst her boyfriend snaps away. She looks again at her phone and isn't happy with the results, she backs away and seems to have the perfect shot in mind. Another handstand follows, this time she spreads her legs so wide I think for a minute I'm back at the Breche de Roland.

As darkness descends, I find a spot just big enough to lie down to bivi, Jim does the same ten metres away.

Nineteen

'I'll go in and ask, they'll know.'

I stand staring at an information board, a description of today's route.

'The GR11 alternative. Faja de Las Olas. Avoid in bad weather, short sections of cable for exposure, some climbing involved. Experienced hikers only.'

Hmm, can it be that bad? It's on the GR11 afterall. After yesterday's chain wedge I could do with a mellow day, maybe just stay here and practice my handstands.

Jim reappears. 'Yep, no problem, we'll be fine just spoke to the girl on reception, she does a lot of climbing and says it's no bother, easy in fact'

'OK. Well let's hope she's one of the few climbers in the world who isn't a complete nutter'

Leaving Goriz, the track skirts near the top of Ordesa canyon with tantalising views of its upper walls. An easy pass is crossed and we hit the junction of the variant and another warning sign. The terrace is high up above skirting around the side of the mountain and out of sight. It's our route for the day and it looks amazing. I'm still a little unsure when four women in their late fifties walk past, they stop at the warning notice and read it briefly. They then continue with all the concern of someone who's just read there's free chocolate on top.

Aniscio

We gently climb 350 metres through a barren landscape, passing a massive herd of sheep bleating manically and into a high cirque, then contour across to the ledge. The Faja high level traverse follows at 2750 metres below the peak Punta de Las Olas. There's distant views out into the Spanish lower lands through the haze to the south but centre stage is Anisclo Canyon. The Bello's river cuts the hills in two and they look like they've been smacked with an axe to separate them. Our traverse carries on around a corner, the river Bello's is now directly below and Punta del Valle, our pass for the day, directly ahead. Vultures funnel through the pass in groups of three or four, they look like fighter squadrons setting off to battle. Sticking close to a cliff and using the thermals to power themselves along, they zip through the gap and swoop just overhead, the wind can be heard ripping through their feathers.

Our little terrace peters out and the Faja de Las Olas begins. It's an easy scramble up a chimney of sorts and the first cable is stretched across the rock face overhead. It's only for three or four metres, so easily traversed. A steep sloping quartz ledge drops from here, another cable dangles for those who want it. Some boulders, another chimney, another down climb and that's it. I wish I'd gone into the refuge now to see what a non nutty climber actually looks like, a once in a lifetime chance missed.

Collado de Anisclo

Now back on main GR11, it's quite busy with backpackers, I was under the impression the GR11 was a fairly easy amble, I am now about to be proved wrong. Standing on the pass I look into the valley below, it seems an insanely steep way down, there is a reason for this, It is. 1200 metres are descended in under two and half kilometres. We drop relentlessly on scree and rock at first, my feet are fighting for grip. Somehow a path has been cut into this slope and is intact. 600 metres of height is lost and a spur is reached with a small spring and I think the worst is over. We enter the tree line, there's a group in front and one of them is struggling badly, she's shakey on her feet and testing every footfall. We pass them and carry on as the track cuts an angle across the forest. A series of down climbs follows, Jim and I are tearing down it but it just keeps on giving. It's gonna be a very long day for the lady behind. Eventually we reach the valley floor and look forward to jumping in the water but there is no river, it's underground. A small stream is crossed before it disappears too. I'm feeling hot and flustered after the last few days and I could really do with a rinse. We find a small pool upstream and lie in it.

As I stand up I spy a strange shape in the trees opposite, it's a belly. The belly has a hand underneath it and its tugging way. Not content with a fiddle of his parts, my voyeur then steps out of the trees in case I missed what he's up to, wearing just a sunhat and socks, it's quite a sight to behold.

I start laughing. Jim looks up.

'Paul , there's a man over there with his togger out watching you.'

'Yep, Ive seen him, Ive always wanted to have sex with a fat naked man wanking in a hedge, shame I'm too tired' ..

We head over to the dry river bed and sit in the sun to dry off and then continue. It's a cruel end to the day with 300 metres of up onto La Ribereta in the afternoon sun. A refuge is marked on the map here but it's closed down and has moved down to the road so we continue to the valley head and put up the tents.

Sick

There's a shudder as bile is once more heaved up into a bucket I'm holding. The ambulance crew have administered an anti sickness drug and it should start working any minute.

'How long has Kaye been sick?'

'The cancer was diagnosed around twenty months ago.' I reply.

'No...how long has she been, being sick.'

'Oh, around four hours, I spent two hour's trying to get the doctor out.'

'OK'. The paramedic is busy typing on to a tablet, more concerned with the report than the patient. I guess they see this sort of thing every day.

The vomiting stops and the ambulance crew pack their things and go. Exhausted, mum is curled up,

'Oh God this is vile.' She says

I hold her hand, 'It'll be alright now Mum'. Here drink some squash, it's that nice grapefruit one.'

I get her toothbrush and as she brushes the white handle of it stands out against her flush skin. She falls into a light sleep, the night before, being a dizzy hell that erupted into vomiting at six am. Looking back from the bedroom door her eyes open.

'Thanks Paulie.'

I smile and turn away quickly, I feel the stress bubble burst as I let go walking down the stairs.

Twenty

The massive bulk of Monte Perdido fills the skyline over the valley. A towering wall, yellow cliffs tumble down from grey mountain tops, a green skirt of trees is scarred by avalanche shoots. Clouds bubble up on the summits but it looks like the weather is settled and it's going to be hot. Trees offer shade for the first hour, a large meadow is skirted around keeping high up on the hillside. A pass of sorts is then crossed and then a big glacial bowl is in front. Rock pinnacles line the edge which then drop 800 metres to the valley floor below. La Estiveta is a magical spot. Once over the final pass, it is a long road plod to Parzan. Now boiling hot, we stop and dunk ourselves in streams that cross the road on the way down. Jim finds a hat so replaces the hat he found on the last walk we did together and puts that one on a post.

'Aren't you going to keep it?'

'I've only got one head.'

There's a big supermarket in town, though it's more geared towards duty free, there's still enough to resupply. I'm hot and thirsty so we walk back out of the supermarket with just two monster size bags of crisps, shopping can wait. A bar over the road has more appeal, being in Spain and on the border it's also very cheap. Oh dear.

We sit and watch people ordering plates of food, great platters of steak, pork chops and chips. We decide to eat later as it's only mid afternoon.

'There's no fags here, three kilometres down the road is the nearest place, I'll get them later.' Jim says, returning from the bar.

The sun is scorching so we sit on the veranda, its shade welcome. The cold beers are delicous.

As the hours drift by we demolish our pillow size bag of crisps, they make us very thirsty. More plates of food pass by, the crisps have regrouped into one massive potato in my gut. I'm now too full to eat this lovely food that keeps passing me, what a feckin eejit.

It's now five pm. 'Jim what about your fags? I'll hitch down and get them ?We can leave the bags here.'

"Can't be arsed, I asked nicely and they sold me some Marlboroughs from behind the bar. '

'What about me? I can't smoke those things, they're vile.'

'Too bad..'

We finish our beers and saunter over to the supermarket to see what time it shuts. Seven.. I then realise tomorrow's Sunday and it's now six forty..Oh shit. Supermarkets in Spain shut dead on time. As we walk in we are told we must be out in five minutes, a mad dash ensues, five days of food, what to get? There's no bread, I panic buy four bags of croissants which have a sell by date of 2030. I'm too drunk to think straight, we randomly chuck food in our baskets almost running down the aisles. Swiss chocolate, pasta, fish. I chuck some disgusting cakes made of marzipan in Jim's basket when he isn't looking.

'What about dinner tonight Jim?'

'More crisps and wine?'

'You must hurry!' The shop manager shouts. He's not helping my fuddled thinking. As we leave I thank him.

'No problem, you forget anything you come back tomorrow morning, we open at eight, we are open every day.'

It must be the only large supermarket in the whole of Spain open on a Sunday. I contemplate taking it all back but the shutter's already down and cars are screeching around the car park and heading home. Sitting in a field on the outskirts of town, we pick through our shopping.

'What the hell are these cakes you made me buy, they look like something you'd wipe the sink with.'

'Its alright for you, I've got croissants that must be made of plastic to have a shelf life this long.'

* * *

TAKING THE HIGH LINE

Tuc Mulleres

Twenty one

The field we've camped in has lovely flat grass, it then dawns on us we could actually be at the end of the garden of a nearby house. We pack early to avoid a confrontation with its owner who will no doubt be sitting on a ride-on mower. I swing on my pack and happen to look down, a camouflage passport holder is half buried in the grass.

'Holy shit! That could have been interesting'. I scoop it up and with it my five hundred euros and passport inside. I ponder, what kind of idiot would buy a camouflage passport holder and then put it down on grass?

The bar in Parzan is open and smells of freshly baked loveliness so we get coffees and a couple of croissants as big as cow horns. The garage next door has a shop which is stocked with food I actually want to eat, I get very excited when I find it has bread and even stocks tomato puree, I think I have finally turned feral. Another coffee is then ordered to celebrate.

The main road is followed out of town for a couple of kilometres we then swing off it and follow a dirt road for the next three hours. We're now reunited with the guidebook so I have a look to recap.

'Tonni says the next eleven kilometres follow a dirt road and GR11. It's very disappointing.'

'Well yes, that's why Tom and I cheated last time.'

Lost in music a 4wd truck pulls up alongside me, I hear shouts so turn around.

'Jump in Paul!'

Jim and Tom are sitting in the back, rucksacks on laps, they've hitched a lift.

'Can't do that, gotta walk the whole way, no cheating!'

'Chuck your rucksack in then, we'll meet you at the top.'

'Err, nah it's alright, me and the bag are enjoying ourselves.'

With that I'm left in a plume of dust as sweat stings my eyes and the pack digs into shoulder blades. Hmm.

The dirt road gently zig zags up, we snake from side to side to avoid the sun, the shadows of trees giving instant relief. The last time I walked up here I put on Bruce Springsteen and stormed it so I do the same. My legs are less storm force these days, more a gentle breeze so I resume plodding up. At the top of Paso de Los Caballos, I turn to Jim and shake his hand.

'Well done you have now walked the entire HRP!'

Jim looks at me for a second with an expression of I couldn't give two shits. 'Whoopity doo' he mutters and makes a cigarette.

It's a long gentle descent through ancient black pines and across high meadows. A fine dust billows up from the path, I've been wearing sandals all day and my feet are as black as coal, the valley floor is reached and I wash them off. My choice of footwear has caused a few raised eyebrows over the years. Germans in particular, almost find it an insult when confronted with someone who looks like they're going to the beach as they are normally clad in great leather boots. One in particular comes to mind that I chatted to in the Alps.

'What is ziss on your feet! You will surely die on this mountain pass. How could you be so reckless?'

I point to some flimsy trainers in the back of my pack.

'I wear these when it gets really bad.'

'But your ankles, you will break zem.'

With that I pad past my interrogator as he stomps on up, each ground shuddering foot fall reverberates behind. Swapping shoes as the day goes on, my feet stay fresh and cool, I can't believe more people don't do it, it also saves on sock washing. Bonus.

The road skirts its way up to Refuge Viados, it's a fine old establishment and we sit in the garden looking at Pico de Posets filling the valley ahead. Small stone barns formerly used for grain and stables litter the valley floor adding to the enchantment of the scene. Further up the valley an old empty cabane sits on a grassy ledge and is the perfect spot for the evening.

Twenty two

I open the tent door and look up the valley. The weather is changing and a storm is forecast to blow in later. Whilst making coffee I warm up croissants on my stove in an attempt to make them more edible. I marvel at how heat resistant they are and change my mind about them being made of plastic and more likely from asbestos.

Our little track heads up a steep sided valley. Posets towers to the right hand side, after an hour, a junction is reached. Our original plan was to keep following the GR11 and have an easier time of it. The HRP takes the highest line for the next few days through mountain cirques and barren rock landscapes. For some reason this seems appealing again this morning, maybe the route around Ordesa has made us crave more high adventure.

A path of sorts follows a stream, it's a steep climb up to Port d'Aiguestortes at 2683 metres, looking down the valley, Lacs de Aiguestortes are dotted on a shelf below and in the distance the Portillion peaks stretch high into the sky. Our way threads a course though them and looks impossible from this angle. The sky is darkening and clouds are heavily pregnant with rain. A steep drop down through rock and scree leads to a flat grassy valley floor, we are now back in France and follow the valley arriving at the unmanned Refuge de Prat-Cazeneuve just after lunch. Our plan is to ride out the storm here, it's a big one forecast to hit the whole of the Pyrenees. Jon Pierre, a young Parisian is already here, he swaggers around the place telling us how quick he is, normally walking two days in one. I'm tempted to tell him he's a bit of a plonker but he realises that we are not really that interested so goes up to his bunk for a snooze. More people arrive, it's only a small refuge and I hate communal sleeping so put up my tent outside which kind of defeats the point of being here .

I lay in my tent reading as distant thunder rumbles. Nick Crane's 'Clear Waters Rising' is a favourite re read, in one particular part of the book as he too walks the HRP, he recounts a particularly gruesome event that happened to the north of here .

> 'Living in the depths of the Grotte de Gargas at the end of the Eighteenth century was an out of work stonemason

called Blaise Ferage, small and broad shouldered, with astonishing strong, long arms. Ferage had got into the habit of eating people. He shot,strangled or stabbed his victims, or dragged them alive to his lair. Unwary milkmaids or passing travellers were taken, although he preferred young women or children. No bodies were ever found. For three years peasants listened through their doors for the crackle of his footfall in the dry autumn leaves, or the rasp of his bloody breath. At night his gleaming eyes pierced the fog. He was, they said, a werewolf.

By 1780 they decided that the cannibal's appetite was getting out of hand and called upon the Parliament of Languedoc to sentence the beast. He was captured but escaped with the help of a talisman hidden in his hair that enabled him to open locks . He was captured again and this time they cut off his hair . But he escaped again. Nobody dare walk the streets. Finally a convicted criminal pretending to flee the law cried for help outside the cannibal's cave. Baise took him in. 'However solitary a man maybe ' wrote Baring Gold ' he yet still craves for the society of a companion...' Baise and the criminal became 'intimate ' and went together on hunting trips. The intimacy didn't last and finally the criminal lured Baise into an ambush. On 12th december 1782, aged twenty five Biase Ferage was convicted of murdering and devouring eight victims and sentenced to death. He was fastened to a cart wheel with his limbs threaded through the spokes . The executioner smashed Baises limbs one by one, then dealt him the coup de grace across his chest.

The storm is now upon us as thunder rumbles overhead and the rain starts to pour. The wind has picked up giving the tent a slap every now and again to make sure I'm still awake. Water starts to puddle around my tent, the ground too dry to suck it up. I begin to question if this was such a good idea afterall as the little rise I'm camped on turns into an island. As long as I don't fall off my scaffold plank thermarest I should be okay. At the very worst, I'll just float down to the lowlands and hopefully make last orders.

The Rain and wind continues through the night, I ram some earplugs in and sleep surprisingly well.

Above Valle Louron

Twenty three

A damp, cold mist hangs heavy in the valley, rumbles of thunder still echo in the distance. After a couple of coffees and more croissant torture it begins to rain again so I go back to sleep. The cloud lifts around lunch time. An easy afternoon is planned so making the complete crossing of the Portillon range a possibility tomorrow. We head off on a high traversing track that was once a narrow gauge railway line, having been blasted into the cliff face, this ledge was part of a massive French hydro scheme in the early twentieth century. It makes for easy progress as the valley floor drops below and we stay fairly level. At the head of the valley, a metal balcony with an odd assortment of rusting train tracks is reached, these disappear behind a large steel door that sits flush with the mountainside, huge pipes drop down the cliff directly below. The whole scene looks like something out of a James Bond movie.

Carrying on around the mountain side we now head up on up Valle Courtalets along another blasted out balcony. A concrete wall is reached blocking the path and rather amusingly you open a door, walk through a derelict building and open another door to continue on towards a big ugly concrete dam that sits broodily in front. Lac de Caillauas is a stagnant mess, its waters low, bits of industrial shite are dotted around as is the skeleton of a large concrete building. I'm quite surprised it has been left like this, the French are normally a tidy lot.

Lac des Isclots restores the tranquility, its green waters a haven to camp beside. From here on it's a land of shattered rock and towering peaks so we pitch up and try to muster up some fortitude for what lays ahead.

Blue Curtain

It's been a long night, I can hear my mother moaning in the next room, the puking has kept me awake for much of it. The past two days have been pretty awful, I've pleaded with her to go to the hospital and get checked out. 'Give it one more day.' she said yesterday. The horror of the previous incarceration is still fresh.

I sit on the end of her bed.

I can't fix you Mum, I'm sorry.'

'I know, it's okay, thanks for trying.'

Two recent hospital appointments to see consultants and it's the same outcome, nothing. The doctors chose to ignore the yellow pallor and arms stretched to pieces, keeping people out of hospital beds, a sad reality of the state of our nation. To suffer at home as long as possible being the preferable alternative. Until you get really ill of course.

The ward is clean and bright, it is in a new wing of the hospital, I'm so relieved to be there. Amanda's here too, having flown from Spain, we sit and chat.

'This bed is ever so comfy- don't let them take it away from me!'

I laugh and walk down the corridor to get a drink and stretch my legs. Walking back into the ward half an hour later, the curtain around the bed is shut, behind it a commotion of noise. I stand and stare at the wall of blue fabric as a man comes out quickly.

The doctor looks at me for a second.

'Your mother has sepsis, I'm sorry.'

Twenty four

An early start is needed today as it's a long one over four Cols but there's a promise of pizza at the end of it, the race is on. After the first rise we enter a world of utter devastation, piles of talus are jumbled high as glacier moraines are picked through and the path is lost, or maybe there just isn't one. Cairns are then followed over slanting rock. We sidle a glacier which has retreated considerably over the last five years, according to reports, the remaining Pyrenean glaciers will all be gone in thirty years. The cairns disappear again so we pick the best line over icy slopes to Col de Gourgs - Blancs at 2877metres.

Col de Gourgs Blanc

Now in a big bowl of crumbling crap, it's a tortuously slow route hopping over boulders to Col du Pluviometre. A rusting rain gauge on stilts sits just above looking like an extra from War of the Worlds. Even in good visibility, route finding is complex here. It's then over to Tusse de Montarque, a large dome of rock at 2889 metres, refuge Portillon is 300 metres below. A big concrete dam holds a bowl of water underneath 3000 metre peaks, I pick my way down slowly to it. Large trout rise to its surface, the refuge restocks the lac and should the guardian catch enough, puts them on the menu for evening meals. The other side of the dam is another high pass, Col Inferieur d Literole and the highest point of the HRP at 2983 metres. The way up is full of scree but a path of sorts is followed. On the way down, a funnel of snow makes for a speedy descent, more picking through barren rock above Lago de Literola leads to another high point where Valle de Remune looks a long way off below. Now the route leads over smooth glaciated ramps which tally with odd splodges of paint. Down we go further and further, it's a maze of rock until the green valley bottom is reached.

Valle Remune

The river Remune cuts a ravine down and is followed, now a proper track has formed but it isn't letting us off lightly as it twists and turns. A down climb passes a waterfall, my water bottle decides it can't take anymore so throws itself out of a side pocket and down into a gorge below. I scramble down and get it as water bottles are hard to come by in these parts. It's all quite beautiful but wasted on me. I'm dreaming of pizza, having eaten sardines and couscous for three nights in a row.

Another hour passes before we are finally spat out on the road, my legs feel like spaghetti. Down in the dip below is the hotel of our dreams, cheap beer and pizza awaits. I sit outside, it's four thirty pm and we've made really good time. Jim appears with 2 halves of beer.

'Erm. I'm not sure what just happened, this seems to be all they serve now.'

I look at the little glasses.

'Where are the big pint tankards..?'

'Oh, and they stopped selling Pizza at four pm.'

I just look at Jim, I'm afraid that if I speak I may start crying. I wait for him to shout 'Sucker!' and a menu to appear but he just looks at me like a man who's been told there's no pizza. It's the saddest sight I've ever seen, Jim's pizza-less expression.

I go inside, it's my turn to confuse the barman. I see a tall glass behind him. 'Fill that one up old fellow.' I gesture .

He passes me a bottle of weird looking beer and the glass. It's made of wheat. Oh well.

Jim finally cracks the code on the next round with a tall glass of Estrella.

There's no one else outside and it's getting dark, this isn't the same experience as last time. Four of us sat in much merriment, empty pizza plates, a table groaning with empty pint glasses and a cacophony of noise from other Spanish walkers. Today it comprises of a cold wind and an empty balcony with two dirty English hikers shivering in the corner as it turns to dusk. It's time to look for somewhere to camp, signs adorn the valley promising hefty fines should you be caught. Earlier I spied some trees that looked like a good spot away from prying eyes so we head towards it. The first obstacle is to cross a small stream, being a bit pissed I try to jump across and land on the oppersite bank at an angle, bouncing back on the rebound I land like an upturned turtle in the middle with water flowing all around and filling my pack, most refreshing.

The spot in the trees is alas, a land of bog so we head to another, it's dark as night by now, probably because it is night. Hunting around by torchlight I remember another place nearer the road so duck into that, it's not ideal but we agree to get up early.

I'm too tired to eat couscous and sardines so decide to have it for breakfast.

Twenty five

Parque Maladeta's a busy place, although traffic is stopped down the valley, buses zoom up and down instead so it's still full of walkers and day trippers. We head up Valle Benasque through ancient pines and arrive at the bus terminus where a cafe and sunshades keep the less energetic amused. Quite a few Spanish are drinking a beer mid morning, I do marvel at their ability to just drink one and continue with their day. For some reason I buy a T-shirt. I don't need one and carry only the minimum amount of stuff. I even weighed my socks before starting to see which ones were the lightest to take. I know, nutter.

We head on up to Plan d'Aiguallut, a wonderful grassy plain surrounded by peaks including the highest in the Pyrenees, Aneto. A popular spot with many families picnicking and enjoying just being here. There's no rubbish either, fancy that. I jump in a deep part of the river, it's fed by a glacier up the valley so jump back out three seconds later.

The crowds are soon left behind as we get up into more remote country. A twisting green valley is the start of our route, it climbs passing many lakes and we are once more in a land of rock. Great bowls have been carved out of granite which makes for smooth walking across a sloping plateau. The sun is beating down as Coll de Mulleres seemly comes into view, I switch on my phone to see how much further it is.

'Jim we've done it again! Gone up the wrong bleeding valley. Mulleres is over the other side of that bloody lump in front.'

Five years earlier, cairns led us the wrong way, we climbed up through swirling mist to a col looking at the cliff below our feet.

'This can't be right? It looks impossible.' I say to Tom.

'Well Paul, it says in the book it's a badass downclimb, though I'm with you on this one.'

I get out the map, something's not right.

'Hang on, why are we looking at a mountain opposite? We should be looking down a valley with a lake at the bottom. I think we are here?' I say, pointing to a col on the wrong side of the 3010 metre peak, Tuc de Mulleres.

'Awesome! We get to do a bonus peak!'

Tom's enthusiasm for extra toil always amazed me, unless it was a gravel road of course. We cross Tuc de Mulleres, it's summit in thick fog, a surreal experience as angles of rock adorn its barren, rocky top poking through the mist. A serrated ridge is followed down the other side to col Mulleres.

Jim and I slowly contour across shattered slopes below Tuc de Mulleres, it's not far but I can't gauge the scale of our surroundings, then, what looks like 100 metres is only 20 and we arrive. I look over the edge, it's a cliff. A proper down climb.

Mulleres

'Wow, I've done a good job in blanking this one out, I don't remember it being this terrifying, that's a long way down.' I try to eat some food but I just want to get it over and done with, I reason with myself that it must not be as bad as it looks or I'd remember... Surely?

A loose chimney is scrambled down, my pack gets stuck so I wiggle and try not to fall forward, falling forward here is a very bad idea. A small ledge is reached, stone is crumbling off and every step is covered in shattered loose rock. The next traversing move is a knee trembler, only a couple of small hand holds to cling to and a void below is stepped across. It's a move of faith to a small foothold, then another to safety. Another shitty loose chimney is descended but it's now on easier ground before a final traverse to the base of the cliff. Jim arrives five minutes later looking a tad shaken.

'That was horrible, I'm sure it was worse than last time.'

We look across at a sea of boulders below and begin picking our way down, it takes hours. By now it's seven pm, a couple walk towards us heading up. Where they plan on sleeping is a mystery, they'll also be going up Col de Mulleres in the dark. A path winds below an orange emergency shelter, the going is easier now but it's still a very long way down. The flat green valley bottom is anything but, being covered in long grass and tussocks. We camp under trees upon dry leaf mould, using flat stones from the river to put our cookers on.

Twenty six

It's a brief walk from here down to Hospital de Vielha, a collection of empty, well kept buildings. Road tunnels disappear into the mountainside with very little traffic using them. The first tunnel took twenty two years to complete and was the longest road tunnel in Europe at 5240 metres long at the time. Being fairly narrow, it was also considered the most dangerous tunnel on the continent, so another much larger tunnel was dug and finished in 2007.

We are now reunited with the GR11 and our super high exploits are over. It's a long snaking track through pine trees to Port de Rue. A stream is crossed and I jump in and rinse my socks that are still on my feet, I'm feeling very lazy as the last few days have been tough going. Once on the open hillside, I look back up the valley at where we came from yesterday. It looks impossible near the top, a cliff rimmed bowl of dazzling rock.

Estany de Rue is disappointing, a large half empty reservoir. A grassy platform halfway along its shores will do for lunch and I chew on stale bread smothered in tomato puree to soften it after a brief dip in the icy waters. Jim scans the horizon and asks what lies ahead as unsurprisingly he can't remember. I look at the guide book and point at a nearby hill.

'Tonni says we should go up over there and look at some other half empty reservoirs...He also states, 'You must not forget one thing, the Haute Route is much more beautiful and spectacular.'

'Tonni tried killing me on Mulleres yesterday, Tonni can go and fuck himself.'

Skirting past a dam, the path drops into another valley, the peaks are beautiful and the river free once more. Then rather rudely we have to climb steeply up towards Refugio Restanca, there's little to distract the brain. Slabs of rock lay hidden under heather making progress slow, the sun is out in full force and is frazzling exposed skin. I stop under a tree and shove the last of my apricots in my mouth.

'Isn't it around here that Tom sat on an ants nest?'

'Ah yes.'

Tom

Tom was an old work colleague that, in turn, became a good friend and Scottish winter mountaineering partner. We have had a few close calls over the years, mostly his fault of course.

He flew out to join me on the first crossing having managed to blag eighteen days leave from his wife, so did a fair chunk of the central Pyrenees with Jim and I. We rendezvous'd in Lescun. Tom had recently embraced ultra light backpacking and had some new kit to use. Luckily the cape that turned into a tarp never materialised but a single skin shelter called a Luna Solo did. Rather crassly I dubbed it the beach shelter the first time he put it up, it was a flimsy looking semi transparent silver triangular tarp.

It had its first real test just out of Gavarnie when an evil thunderstorm had tumbled into the high valley where we were camping. Fingers of cloud as dark as night began to consume the mountainside and as it edged closer, the temperature dropped. There seems to be a stand off at first then. Boom! The first gust of wind hit our tents head on, then another, much stronger this time from behind, it felt like the oxygen from the valley was being sucked out and was feeding the monster rising up in front. You know you're in trouble when this happens ... Brace yourself here it comes... The air then turns cold for a second, a flash so bright, fires through your retinas and burns a couple of holes in the back of your head. Thunder shudders the ground; a sonic wave causes a mini tsunami of phlegm through your lungs, then a terrific wind ladened with hailstones slams into the tents.

My single hoop tent creation twists and flexes, slapping me on the face as I frantically move the cooker from the concave nylon as flames leap wildly . Jim holds onto his like a parachute, arms threaded through the inner tent webbing. If his flimsy pegs fail, he'll be launched up into space in his red socks saying. 'There's no place like home, there's no place like home.'

I hear a shout from the beach shelter.

'I'm in my waterproofs guys, rucksack's packed.. Woah!..I've just realised my walking pole makes the perfect lightning conductor!'

Another slap of wind from the back and rain falls so heavy it sounds like a machine gun. For a minute the sky is a waterfall, it then turns back to hail. Lightning cracks off in random directions, going mental for a bit and then suddenly peters out.The rumbles become more distant and fade. Outside the floor is covered in malteser size hailstones, a chink of light breaks the darkness .

We have survived, we get out of tents to watch our attacker go and terrorise some cows in the valley below. The Luna Solo as it turns out, has great wind shedding properties. Tom is so enamored with it he makes a video that gets 43000 hits on YouTube.

Jim's tent has snapped a pole and sags like wilted lettuce.

Tom in his beach shelter

Crossing a large concrete dam, the refugio is a hive of activity. A waterfall opposite comes to life as if there's a flash flood and walkers staying for the night eagerly take photos. It takes a minute to work out what's going on. The reservoir above is feeding this one, filling up this body of water so it too can be released to create power. It creates the impression of an over scaled, garden centre water feature.

There's one final steep climb to the cheerily named Lac du Deth Cap, a pretty little lake nestled in a bowl of mountains, its natural shoreline evoking peace and solitude, perfect reflections of surrounding peaks are mirrored in the lake. A fisherman slowly circumnavigates the lake and catches nothing, I don't think he's too bothered. Trout bobble up near our tents as I get creative with the last of my food.

Lac du Deth Cap

Twenty seven

We set off early for Coll de Crestada, I decide to pick up water on the way up but the stream disappears underground so arrive at the top thirsty. Ahead is Parc Nacional d'Aiguestortes, a high plateau of mountain lakes and peaks, we skim the top of this little paradise for only an hour unfortunately and head to Port de Caldes 2560 metres. I sit on top of the pass and feel weak, I think mountain scurvy is setting in as I dream of bananas, oranges or just a carrot.

The valley down is quite beautiful, before turning a corner to another half full reservoir, being a road head there's a lot of tourists. We descend through pines, across meadows, it's all very pleasant and sheltered from the midday sun. Jim and I are on a mission having missed the pizzas a couple of days ago. There's a bar and hotel half way down the valley that sells big burgers and barbecues them to order. I arrive and it looks very different here than five years ago. The little tapas bar has become a bistro, no more barbeque, no more burgers. We sit in the corner feeling a bit out of place and grimy cupping a beer but that's also doubled in price from our last visit.

A long road walk follows and for a couple of hours we trudge on tarmac with the heat pressing down. Soon a quiet shady garden attached to a pension will be our reward but for now there's little else to do except force legs into a speed march. Jim carries on along the tarmac as I cut off a few bends and get in front, I can sense his annoyance as he manages a crafty manoeuvre on a long curving stretch of tarmac nearly beating me, only to be confronted by a high fence. I hear his distant obscenities as I victoriously pull ahead once more.

Salardu comes into view, the town is built on a small hill and I can hear music playing as I head up to the main street. Turning a corner, I'm confronted by a sea of Stetsons, I stand on the spot blinking as this is not something you see everyday. A big banner barricades the road.

Salardu Festival Country Rock Entrada.

Spanish wannabe cowboys, pot bellied and semi retired is the general demographic, all in identikit ten gallon hats, spray on jeans, white shirts and cowboy boots that make normal walking impossible. The ladies are dressed the same, although their pot bellies are smaller, they can't walk in their boots either. It's baking hot and everyone looks uncomfortable and unsure of what to do next. A few marquees are set up and someone inside is murdering a Willie Nelson song. I find the whole thing rather amusing as it's always a great feeling to hit town after a week in the wilds. For some reason I wasn't expecting a fancy dress cowboy festival though, silly me. We thread our way through stalls selling belt buckles, stetsons, leather jackets, T-shirts emblazoned with eagles, American flags and of course cowboy boots complete with chromed toes. There's even North American Indian memorabilia to channel your inner Tonto, like Dream Catchers, 'you've taken our land, now let us take your dreams.'

Arriving at the cheap pension in town, we're convinced it'll be full but they have room. Turns out a cowboy's budget is bigger than a hobo's.

Achy Breaky Heart

Salardu only has a small shop so we catch a bus down to Vielha, being a Sunday the big supermarket is shut but there's another small one to check out, it's not up to much unfortunately but will do for today. I take a walk around town trying to find the old Vielha, there's not much left, most of it feels fairly modern. It used to be a forgotten place cut off from Spain with the only mountain road getting blocked by snow in the winter. They then of course built the tunnel and that changed everything, now it's a ski town of sorts. On my second circuit of its streets, I bump into Jim so we find a local bar and go for a beer. We're both a bit jaded so just have one and catch the bus back to Salardu.

The wannabe cowboys are still milling around. It must be the most uninteresting music festival ever organised, I mean where's the music? At the far end of the village is a large boxing ring, it has around thirty people in there line dancing and at least fifty watching. I open a beer and take it all in. Cow folk in all shapes and sizes, happily dancing, who'd have thought it?.. And they haven't even played Billy Ray Cyrus yet, I bet they all go mental when that comes on. I become mesmerized, the flow and waggle of hips turning to the music is very trippy, kind of like watching a shawl of fish all moving in time stamping their fishy feet and clapping their fishy fingers. Fish with Stetsons on...I think for a second maybe I should get a Stetson and then I think I've been thinking far too much lately..

A famous country and western band are playing tonight, I try and sneak in but all the entrances are guarded but it doesn't really matter though, I can hear it perfectly. Songs about poking cows and chasing girls. 'Yes siree, you alls the best audience. Ooo eee! Ain't that so Jimmybob?'

With that I leave.

* * *

BACK OF BEYOND AND BACK AGAIN

Tuc de Marimanya

Twenty eight

It's an early bus back to Vielha, we need a week's food for the next section so it's worth waiting for the big supermarket to open after the last shopping experience in Parzan. I try to make my meals interesting. Six carrots, a half a kilo tube of guacamole, cooked mini pizzas, some tomatoes, onions and a few bananas. Then all the usuals, muesli, noodles, canned fish, couscous, eggs, dried fruit and nuts, peanut butter, a mountain of bread, avoiding anything that looks like a packet of croissants.

By the time we're back in Salardu and packed, it's lunchtime and hot. An hour of road walking follows to Bagergue, flopping onto a bench and dripping with sweat, I watch Jim walking up the road into the village. Why am I even doing this? I feel myself waning, loaded down with another week's food and at least another sixteen days to go. I look down the valley at Salardu and take out my frustration on a carrot.

'Good carrots these Jimmy.' I say, 'aren't we happy bunnies today..?'

Jim gives me a toothless smile, what teeth he has left probably couldn't deal with a raw carrot so I don't offer him one.

Pull the other one

I'm not sure if Jim actually blames me for his lack of teeth but it was my fault we got lost which led to his incisors departing a few years ago in the Italian Alps. We were following the Grande Traversata delle Alpi on the Italian border and had walked off the end of our last map. The guide book had been quite adequate so far, it contained a simple outline map and as it was a well signposted route we decided to carry on mapless. This was fine until we missed a signpost, we press on regardless up and over a hill to a wide valley cutting across our path, this was a little odd as a valley wasn't supposed to be there. We take a look at the guide book map.

'Oh maybe it's this stream Jim? It looks much smaller on here..Hmm, that means we went up this track then..'

I say this whilst pointing at a map so devoid of information it would probably get you lost in a supermarket. I dig out my compass like a good boy scout. 'This'll tell us if it's the right way'...and then say the immortal and sometimes deadly words,'this compass is wrong', as its direction arrow points the oppersite way.

Jim looks up the valley. 'Well I can see people up there - it goes somewhere.'

An hour later we arrive at the top of a pass and a sign welcomes us to Col d Urine. We have arrived in France. Being in France is not ideal when you're supposed to be walking in Italy so we do the sensible thing and have lunch. If being mildly lost isn't bad enough Jim takes a bite out of his stale baguette, mindlessly pulling on it like a dog with a stick and his front tooth pops out.

'Oh Sit!.' He says it with a slight whistle and an inability to pronounce consonants.

'Wollox!'

I then notice his other front tooth is wobbling as he exhales.

'Err, I'm afraid that one's days are numbered too.'

It comes out with a little wiggle.

'Maybe with the money you make from the tooth fairy we can get a taxi back to Italy?'

'Wiss off you wanker'.

'It's not all bad Jim, at least you can smoke now without having to open your mouth.'

Jim lets out a whistle that a minute eariler would have been a sigh.

Some French day walkers are nearby so I ask if I can look at their map to see where the hell we are. I take photos of it and we take a long trackless route skirting high back to Italy.

An old mountain track cuts up the hill from the village, now on an open hillside a four wheel drive track contours around high above a series of new ski villages in the valley below. There seems to be a lot of money being spent in this valley, none of it looks particularly appealing to a non-skier. A few ski tows are then passed before at last heading uphill into an ancient pine wood and back to the high country. Once out of the trees, I take delight at seeing the rolling plateau with wild horses in front, the two high mountain lakes of Rosari need to give us little persuasion to stay, so we set up camp. Not a long day but we are on the move and in real cowboy country at last.

Twenty nine

Tuc de Marmimanyna rises up to greet us, we decide to stick to the proper route this time up through the middle of the hill. Our last visit saw us take different more 'interesting' lines to its summit. I took the ridge on the right, it looked a nice way up and indeed it was until the last 500 metres, a series of giant flat slabs shaped like cream crackers lay jumbled at angles, I crawled crab like over one of them, it was the size of a sheet of plasterboard and rocked towards me rather alarmingly as I pull up and pad my way over it. I had visions of it toppling back whilst I hung on and being flattened like a popped tomato. Once on top, I was surprised not to see Jim as he took a more direct route up a gully. Whilst admiring the view I hear a scream, then silence.

That's not good, I think to myself, I scamper down the rocks and fear the worst. He must be badly injured or dead, what's even worse is he's just ruined my holiday. Some people are so bloody selfish.

A bold head pops up above a rock. 'Lost me bloody hat!'

'I thought you were dead, you pillock!. Oooh, what's happened to your leg?'

A large scrape down the shin is gently oozing blood.

'The gully got steep and loose, I slipped and then got stuck, that's when my hat fell off and I scratched my leg..'

The way up the middle was a doddle after that. Tuc de Marmimanyna is 2662 metres high and has a commanding view, a series of peaks filling the horizon stretching out to the east. The next few days are going to be wild and remote, I'm filled with excitement but first we have to get past the boulder field of hell below. The broad valley is chock full of boulders and there's nothing else for it but to start hopping. It's torturously slow going, each one a leg breaker if you get it wrong and even the biggest rocks can catch you out with a wobble. It starts to drizzle, making our hopping even more precarious as the rocks become greasy. We contour high above a lake and eventually reach Col de Moredo at 2420 metres.

I dig out my bucket of guacamole, there must be at least ten avocados squashed in there. It's delicious with fresh tomatoes and onions. As the days go on all the fresh veg and fruit gets eaten but the guacamole keeps giving, even after nearly a week of baking in the back pack, the last scrapings are still green. I try not to think about what preservatives are doing this but look on the bright side that if I ingest enough of them maybe I'll stay forever young, or more likely just look like a giant avocado.

A good path leads down to the Estany Moredo and continues through a long valley before dropping to a dirt road, a path cuts off the road's corners. 1100 metres of descent later a river is reached and then an old drovers track leads into Alos de Isll, Its narrow cobbled streets lead to a main square where we have lunch number two.

The earlier cloud has burnt off and it's getting hot. A beer barrel and pump are stacked in the corner of the square next to a marquee.

'Do you think it works Jim?'

'Only one way to find out.'

The barrel was empty, just as well really, it would have been hard work carrying it for the next week. Before we set off I jump in a massive stone drinking trough with all my clothes on, it's warmed by the sun so it's the perfect temperature to rinse off the day's grime. I clammer out and start packing my lunch away as an old lady walks through the square and dips her hand into the trough, scooping up a couple of handfuls of water, she quenches her thirst. She makes a gurgling noise with the water before swallowing and then walks past us smiling, obviously very pleased to have just sampled 'soupe du jour a la Paul'

The next half an hour is along a road gently uphill, by the time we reach our turning, my wet clothes are as dry as a bone. It's a long, slow pull up and the evening shadows grow as a number of camping spots appear to tantalise investigation, only to be completely covered in cow shit. Higher up, a green meadow flattens out, home to a dozen cows. We pick a patch of flat grass as young bullocks watch our every move. Noodles and sardines are quickly cooked as the sunsets over our day's endeavours.

Thirty

Above the meadow we sit on the shore of Bass a de Sobriu, a small lake in a green bowl and have a second breakfast. For the next four hours the HRP winds its way above 2000 metres across scree and rock, passing numerous lacs and over three cols. Cairns mark the route but as ever in Spain, they are not to be trusted, having gone astray here last time. At Col Cornella it's a short drop to Estanys Tartena then across a natural bowl staying high to Col Curious. The path skirts around threading a course to a gap in the mountains in front. I stop at the next lake and jump in, it's a cold, quick swim and I shiver uncontrollably when out. Refreshing? Yes. Invigorating? Nope. It takes half an hour for my feet to defrost upon arriving at Col de Calberante. We then enter the high cirque of Los Vedos on the other side.

Los Vedos

Four lakes are stepped below, the route twists between each one over rolling orange granite slopes, a beautiful bowl in the heart of the mountains. Ahead on the opposite shore of Lac Gallina, a small refugio beckons us in. There's no one else here so we take a break, looking through the accumulation of what people leave behind because they can't be arsed to carry it back down. Burnt out night lights, a dribble of wine in the bottom of the bottle, an empty gas canister, some spaghetti..there's always half a packet of spaghetti. Oh and of course, a cube of Bovril.

In the corner of a bunk lies an old sleeping bag and tucked in it a bizarre type of tupperware container with a locked lid. It's quite heavy so I try to open it, I twist and pull at the lid but it won't open.

Jim looks across impatiently .'Give me a go.'

He twists and turns it, giving it some welly. Then.. POP!!

Somebody's rice and chickpea dinner scatters across the wooden floor.

'Oh shit!

'Oh Shit!' I reply.

'What shall we do?'

'Get out of here!'

We scrape it up, bits of detritus invariably end up in there too and indeed anything else that happens to be on the floor of a well used hut. We pick out what we can see. I have to say I feel bad about it and hope they won't notice the odd bit of fluff, grit or a mouse dropping or two.

We head down past a waterfall into another glorious valley following a river over yet more smooth, glaciated rock and continue to Noarre. A hamlet that comprises of clusters of barns and a few little cottages nestled together on the side of a grassy hill. It's like a lost village, smart but seemingly abandoned. An old drovers track leaves the little village. Tired legs are pushed up hill for another 500 metres snaking our way through birch trees to eventually arrive at a small grassy plain high up on the mountainside. A gentle river running through it makes for an idyllic spot to spend the night.

Little Portions

'Not too much now.'

'Yep, I know.'

I hear a familiar shout from the living room, the same thing having been said for the last few weeks. I Plate up one dinner on a large saucer. I have to get creative to get the fat content up, butter under the peas and potatoes, cook the chop a bit greasy, rich gravy. I bring it out on a tray.

'Oh, thank you.'

Meal sizes have been getting steadily smaller. Food is becoming a chore as appetites shrink. We sit and watch The Chase. Bradly Walsh is a distraction and as usual, we try to answer the questions first.

'I've nearly eaten it all.'

A lonesome potato sits on the plate, I head to the kitchen with it. Mum goes up stairs to put on her pyjamas at six pm as she starts to feel itchy after dinner. It's amazing what starts to feel normal in a short space of time.

Thirty one

Sitting on the banks of Estany Guerosso, an hour's walk above last night's camping spot, I watch the horses happily frolicking in the sun.

Jim joins me. 'Ah so there they are, I thought they'd have been eaten by now.'

These may or may not be the same horses but when camping on the plain below, they gave us hell on our last visit. Waiting until the tents were pitched, they then came over and stuck their heads in our tents trying to eat our food. Sitting in a tent with six foot of horse above you is a little disconcerting to say the least. My patience ran out when one stood on my tent.

We decamped to a highpoint on a ledge above. The horses of course saw us and followed, waving and shouting wouldn't stop them. I took this as a declaration of war, so armed with stones we proceeded to launch our attack. It didn't take long, a few well placed rocks on the rump of the ringleader had them running back down to the meadow. An hour later they came back up. We re-armed and let them have it this time. They never came back.

'Do you think they remember us?'

'You probably smell the same.'

Our route for the day now continues up and over the scree-covered Col de Certascan 2605 metres and then down through red shattered rock to a dammed lake and onwards to Refugi Certascan. We ponder the pros and cons of sharing a bottle of wine but drinking at lunch time is never a good idea, not unless you just keep on drinking of course. Somehow we see sense and another long descent follows. Our days of up down then up again seem set to continue as we drop 1200 metres crossing green meadows and through pine forests to Pla de Boavi. River Lladorre offers a surprisingly cold dip and a lunch break.

From here it is a long afternoon of uphill, starting in a pine forest, we weave our way, the track shaded thankfully. We share pleasantries with a young Dutch guy who is sitting on a rock. He catches us up around the halfway mark, Han's is walking the HRP too, so we fall in line talking the usual waffle and slowly chew off the last part of the 1100 metres of ascent to Col de Selente. A small unmanned refugio is on the other side of the pass but people can be seen milling around outside so we head to the lake shore and camp. Sitting outside our tents and cooking, Hans starts talking.

'I'm on a mission, I spoke to a guy coming the other way, he says there's a man in front, he's a legend, apparently he hands out free marajuana... I need to catch up with him and smoke his weed!'

'Ahh, you mean Majeed?'

'YES! You know him? A Moroccan with a bag full of hash. I've heard he's only a day in front of us'

'We met him on the first day.'

'Have you got any?'

'You won't believe this but I refused it, I kind of wish I hadn't now though.'

Hans looks at me for a few seconds.

'You refused….Free hash?.'

'I know...Well it was very strong but I did think we'd see him again, we crossed paths a few times at the beginning..'

'Well the guy I met gave me some, Man it's so good, shall we smoke it?'

'Go on then, make it weak. I don't feel like going to sleep just yet.'

We sit under the stars drinking tea, the hash makes us giggle at anything. It never crossed my mind at the time to make a weaker spliff until now, oh well, at least I can remember the last four weeks.

Thirty two

Deep blue skies greet the day along the shores of Estany de Baborte. A winding path through pines drops 600 metres past the solitary Cabane Bastallo then to the river and road. A long, gentle climb follows crossing meadows and open forest. As we climb higher, another higher plateau is entered. Ahead a man with a shiny, shaved head is walking towards us holding a piece of paper.

'I'm not sure where I am, please show me?'

I take a look at his map, it's a confusion of contours at best and looks like it was photocopied from a map made in the 1940's.

'Erm, I don't think you're on it., where are you going?'

'My car is here, near Ent's.'

I get out my phone and have a scan around.

'Ahh yes that's in Andorra, it's the next valley. You need to go back up and over the pass, the way you've just come from.'

'No, I want to go this way.' Shiny head says. He is starting to get irritated

'Well if you do, you'll get to a road, the road goes a very long way out of the hills before getting to the valley where your car is. '

'No, no. I go this way!'

'It's the wrong way.'

'Pah!'

I turn to Jim.

'Can't help some people.' I say and watch the shiny head disappear down the wrong valley.

'Oh well, let the plonker get down to the refuge, he can then pay for a very expensive taxi.'

We climb further to Estanys de Baiau, a lake surrounded by jagged, shattered peaks with purple and red pink hues in the rock. It forms a high amphitheatre and the frontier with Andorra. There's a faint route to the far end of the lake, then it's across boulders to a chimney of scree. The scree makes for hard work which is not helped by the fact I'm wearing my sandals, I change to trainers and continue up the steep slog to the top of Port de Baiau 2757 metres. The view has been stifled out as the sky darkens, distant thunder rumbles and echoes around. The air feels electric.

Port de Baiau

'I think we best get out of here Jimmy.'

Our track drops to a small, bouldery lake and then cuts across the hillside, down below is a hanging valley with the Refugio Pedrosa just above on a bluff. As ever, it's a lot further to get to than it looks.The storm that was brewing gets pushed into another range of hills, we can still hear it booming down the valley next to ours as we stick up our tents and head up to the refugio.

'I've just been bollocked by a dreadlocked hippy! He said we shouldnt be camping down there, it's forbidden. I had to say sorry, lots, otherwise he'd have made us take our tents down. When you go in, say your sorry too.'

' Yeah right, to a power crazed dreadlocked hippy? He can sod off.'

'He also said we can only camp there as long as our tents are down by 7am. I said OK.'

'Well that's good Jim, you'll get a nice early start whilst I lie in bed eating breakfast.'

We sip our wine, considering we haven't drank for five days, neither of us are really up for it. I go inside to get another to have with dinner anyway. People staying in the refugio are deadly quiet. In the kitchen no one's speaking, I spy the man with dreadlocks.

'Another wine please' I say chirpily . 'Can you stick it in this?' as I give him a plastic bottle.

'Sure.'

The silence is deafening as the wine glugs into the bottle. He seems to be waiting for me to say something, I just keep grinning inanely and hand over the money. Back down at the tents we happily make dinner and wonder where our shiney headed friend is right now.

Thirty three

I hear rustling, it's six forty five am, Jim's all packed by seven as I open my tent door.

'Well done Jim, nice to see you're a man of your word, I'll just finish my coffee and breakfast and be with you.'

By seven thirty we're away. A soft morning light filters through mountain pines, we drop down steeply and then contour high above the Andorran valley with the town of Arinsal spread out below. It looks like a confusion of newly built holiday apartments, roads and shops from here, thankfully way out of reach. An ugly ski run compliments the scene on the hillside opposite.

The track passes through woodland and links up small farming hamlets as it winds its way. It's starting to get hot just in time for the next two hours of uphill. Pic del Clot de Cavall at 2587 metres looms above and is a long, slow, sweaty pull uphill to reach its summit. From the top, peaks stretch in all directions, it is a fine view indeed. Another knee crunching descent follows past lakes and a high mountain plateau. It feels a million miles from the mass of Andorra below. It's then a long drop through forest to Llorts, a little village in the valley. The track is heavily wooded so Llorts quite suddenly appears and within minutes I'm sat in a small square. I ditch five days worth of empty, festering sardine cans in a bin, the smell seems to linger, you are what you eat, so they say, I chuck some water on the most offending parts and pat down my hair. One must keep up appearances.

Alas, things have changed here in five years. The campsite is closed and with it the promise of a shower and fresh bread in the morning is no more. To make matters worse, the old locals bar we frequented last time is also shut, along with it, the option of insanely cheap beer and food. It seems old Llorts is being redeveloped and with it, the campground which looks destined to become a block of ski chalets.

Sitting under an umbrella outside an expensive restaurant, the rain gently drizzles as beer is supped, we are both too tired to think straight, feeling jaded and miserable.

'I was looking forward to coming here. No campsite. No bread. No pub.'

'I know. And no fags!'

Thirty four

I hear a dog sniffing around my tent, its owner shouts something in Catalan, probably along the lines of 'keep away Patch or you'll catch something bad.' We are camped on the edge of a park next to the river on the outskirts of Llorts. It's a cool morning, I would attempt a wash but the water's freezing. We pack up and head up to El Serrat, an hour's walk away, for a coffee. The path up the valley follows the road on the opposite side of the river. At El Serrat it starts to drizzle again, all hotels and bars with outside seating are shut, the fondness I once had for Andorra is rapidly diminishing.

Leaving the village a tour group of American walkers approach from the opposite direction, we nod hellos as the rain steadily falls. Further on, I come across a Nalgene water bottle on the path, these are the Rolls Royce of walking bottles, wide necked and indestructible. I pick it up and shove it in a side pocket of my pack, it must have been dropped by the group earlier I surmise. I regret picking it up soon afterwards as I don't need it and it's heavy, I vow to leave it at the next refuge we pass- by mistake. The rain eases and moods improve as a wide meadow and closed refugio is passed. The river offers fine bathing so I scrub and wash. I'm clean again!

Collanda dels Meners at 2713 metres is crossed and briefly we enter a land of rock and scree before it turns green again as we drop once more. The higher hills are now back and so are my sweaty armpits. I'm dirty again!.

Descending steeply to a lac, the sky begins to darken and cloud spills in from the north, our little path contours a high line and brings us to Cabana Coms de Jau as the first rumbles echo in the next valley over. In the cabane a small group of middle aged Germans do their best to be as unfriendly as possible.

We walk down to a stream a few hundred metres below the cabane as horses idly feed on the slopes around us. Tents are thrown up as the cloud drops further, the storm is almost upon us, I lie on the scaffold plank tensing up and wait as the temperature drops.

I shout across.

'This could be bad Jim.'

WHITE LIGHT. BOOOM!!

'That was less than a second, probably two hundred metres away.' Jim replies.

'Let's hope it took out the cabane with those grumpy fuckers inside.'

'Or maybe a horse, I could eat a horse right now.'

FLASH! BANG! WALLOP!

'Holy shit, the ground just shook!'

The rain hits hard, it's so loud on the nylon fly it drowns out the thunderstorm going mental above us. The stream below rapidly fills and has now burst its banks, the hillside above a running mass of water. As I lie down I attempt reading but I can hear a gurgling sound under my head, there's a dip in the ground directly underneath my pillow and water is starting to seep through the ground sheet. I put on waterproofs and drag the tent up the slope. Repegged, I clamber back in. Considering the noise the storm is making, the horses on the other side of the stream look pretty nonplussed and continue grazing as the rumbles of thunder continue into the evening.

Incoming storm Cabana Coms de Jau

Thirty five

I wake up with wet feet, having slid down the tent, my feet are wedged in the dip that was under my head during the storm. Outside all is calm, the waters have receded, the air is cool and damp as we pack. The first hill crosses a ridge line in thick fog then a steep descent to Caban de Sorda which is next to Estany de Cabana Sorda. Looks like they have run out of names around here. Our track drops slowly on a diagonal to another valley and as we round a corner, a group of walkers approach us. I hear an American accent so stop to talk to the leader.

'Did we pass you near El Seratt?'

'By golly yes indeed, you sure did.'

'Anyone lose a water bottle a few days ago?'

'Frank over there.'

I reach back and pull out the bottle from a side pocket.

'Here you go Frank.'

Frank looks stunned, reunited after two days, he stares at the bottle then at me and then the bottle again.

'Be more careful next time, there's a good lad.'

With that we disappear back into the mist, I hear distant laughter and a lady saying 'Oh my Gawd, oh my Gawd'. Frank's wife no doubt.

Good deed done, a high valley is dropped into, the wind is still cold. Sheltering behind trees, we pick at our food, it's been seven days since our last re-supply. I look into my food bag, there's not a lot to be cheerful about in there, mashed crackers and peanut butter are complemented by a week old boiled egg.

It's a gentle climb to Port de Fontargente and with it, we are back in France where we'll stay pretty much until the end. The cloud is still floating around as we push on past Fontargente lakes, the path then skirts a boulder field as mist coats and dampens. Refuge de Rulhe sits above somewhere as Jim heads off at a pace and I stop to photograph a rock, more an excuse for a rest than having any artistic merit.

I flop on a bench outside the refuge next to Jim's pack and idly pick at some sultanas whilst looking at the map. Our route goes through Hospitalet Andorre tomorrow, a nondescript village wedged between a busy road, train line and powerstation. It has no shop either so I look for alternatives.

'Look what I've got. Mulled wine!'

'Crickey, are we that slow it's Christmas already?'

We sit and sup, it's a warming spicy syrup that's very comforting and a real taste sensation after such a bland lunch.

'This is delicious. Like a Malbourgh, Paul?'

'I can't face Hospitalet tomorrow, let's follow the GR10 to Merens and get the train to Les Cabannes, we can resupply and slob out for a day or two.'

'Good idea.'

Thirty six

The air is cool and the sky bright as we wind our way over a small pass and contour below Pic de Hulhe and Fourcade, Etang Blu sits below still in shadow. It's then up to the highest point of the day Pyramide de Lherbes at 2438 metres, Jim for some strange reason decides to stop five minutes from the top for an early lunch. I join him for a bit but as I don't really have anything worth the effort of eating, I push on to the top.

My phone has been playing up and hasn't worked at all in Andorra as no data roaming agreement has been made with the EU, it also says I have no credit left. I still have £20 on it to top up, so I decide to do that in the village below as it looks like we'll get there in the early afternoon. It's a very long drop down of 1400 metres on snaking zig zags at first. I begin to fantasize of fruit, of tinned peaches, of anything actually with a natural flavour and with it my speed increases. Tearing down into a high valley and then to an old stone lined drovers road shaded by trees, I pass other day walkers at full tilt.

'Bonjour, bonjour, bonjour.' I holler, sounding a tad crazed.

As I enter Merens de Val, I quicken my pace even more to the busy main road, trucks and cars whizz by, a row of dirty fronted houses line the road. It's a ghost town, no shops, bars or cafes, nothing. At the far end of the village there's a train station where I sit in the shade and watch a train arrive and then leave, there isn't another one for three hours. 'Where the fucks Jim?' I mutter to myself as the train trundles down the valley. I'm desperate for a cool drink and chug down some warm water. I try again to top up my phone but it's not having it.

Forty minutes later my phone pings. 'Where are you?'

Then in horror I see the £20 credit has disappeared.

I find Jim on the main road.

'Your text just cost me twenty quid!. And this village sucks...Let's hitch.'

We walk to the end of the village, Jim goes first.

'Jimmy don't grin, you look like an escaped convict, tidy yourself up man.'

'Piss off.'

Ten minutes pass, no cars even slow down.

'Ok it's my turn, this is how you do it Jim, watch and learn.'

'Yeah right. Twat.'

I stick out my thumb as the first car approaches, it stops.

'If you've got it shake it baby!'

'Oh piss off!'

We pile in the back of the car, rucksacks on laps. Once in, our saviours quickly open the front windows and light cigarettes to mask the smell, hardly surprising. They tell us they drive to Andorra every three weeks to fill up with fuel, alcohol and fags. The money they save is enough to buy lunch when they are there and have a jolly day out.

Les Cabannes has all we need, a shop, a campsite and a shady square to sit in and eat. The evening and next day are spent rotating between these three places, I feel a wave of tiredness here and could happily stay for the week. The last section of the walk has been hard work .

Black Hill

'Take my photo Paul and send it to Mandy!'

Mum is grinning, elated at getting out and walking. The Black Mountains are on her right hand side, the rolling hills of Herefordian countryside just below on the left. We are on her favourite walk. Black Hill or the Cats Back, forms the Welsh border. A place that has seen much coffee and Welshcake consumption over the years. The walk didn't look like it would happen the day before but for some reason the dizziness caused by the chemotherapy three months ago has eased off and we are free as birds on the ridgeline.

We get to the top and get out the flasks.

'Well I couldn't believe it'. Mum starts saying.

'I felt so well and when he said I had to have more Chemo I could have died. 'So I'll have to give it a go, I have no other choice really do I?' I look at her and she smiles. 'So we'll see.'

We head down into the valley. I glance back at her and she's looking around taking her time. I wonder if we'll ever do this again together or if this will be the last time.

It is.

❈ ❈ ❈

AN ENDING ON LAST LEGS

Puig Neulos

Thirty seven

It's a grey morning as the train pulls alongside. We board and look out the window as the French countryside flashes by. The ticket office at the station was closed and the conductor is nowhere to be seen, I'm not particularly worried but Jim fidgets like a man with a suitcase of cocaine at an airport. We stand and watch the train pull away at Merens de Val. I reason with Jim that they didn't charge us as, who the hell wants to get off here?

'It could be worse, you know?'

'How's that?'

'We could be in Hospitalet Andorra.'

'Not so sure really. At least it had a bar.'

I ended my first crossing of the HRP at Hospitalet. A confusion of dates meant I also started the walk here and in doing so walked the last section to the Mediterainean first (bear with me) I then went to the start at Hendaye on the Atlantic coast and then walked back to Hospitalet. The Americans call it flip flopping, doing certain sections of a long trail in a different order, normally to allow for snowfall or when the weather is better. The reason I did it was so I could meet Tom on a certain date in Lescun and also finish the walk by the 31st of August in time for an important birthday. That final evening in Hospitalet, Jim's friend Dave arrived from the UK with two litres of home made vodka. I forget what happened after that but do remember waking up in an empty marquee after sleeping on tarmac in the village car park.

The track picks its way through the village and leads to the GR10. From there we head up a valley following a river, a hot spring bubbles next to the path complete with a muddy looking hippy sat in it. After a few hours the trees thin as we pass Estagnas, a small lake surrounded by a high cirque of mountains. The climb is fairly mellow, the weather cool as clouds float lazily overhead. Porteille des Besines at 2333 metres is then crossed. As we drop down, three ladies are feverishly painting GR markers on trees, rocks and anything that doesn't move. There were markers every twenty metres, I don't think they fully understood the brief.

Refuge des Besines is a busy place, it's the first refuge I've ever seen that charges for camping plus there's lots of signs telling you not to do things. I'm not keen on the place so we carry on up the valley to a kink in the river and a small meadow hidden from view. Perfect.

Thirty eight

Crossing Col de Coma de Anyel the landscape changes abruptly, high steep sided mountains give way to more distant hills and open valleys. The high frontier ridge is left for a couple of days, being broken by a high wide plateau, part of the Catalanes Pyrenees National Park. Dropping down past Lac Lanoset to a remote cabane, Peak Carlit towers in front with the massive Etang de Lanoux filling the valley below

'Fancy going up there Jim?'

'No thanks.'

'Good.'

Jim walks on in front up to a shallow pass and into the next valley, as I try to catch up I spy something glinting on the floor nearby. A monocular, wow! Something actually worth finding I think to myself. I look through it to a distant peak, the peak is still distant so I turn it the other way just in case, nope not that way either. It has no zoom, it is completely useless.

I catch up with Jim and hand it to him.

'What's that then?'

'Here Jim you have it, a gift from a friend.'

'Ooo. Thank you.'

'Have a look at the peak over there.'

'Hmmm. Maybe I should try it the other.....Hmm.'

Thanks Paul. But I couldn't, you're just too generous.'

'I think it was lost by someone near Hendaye and has been picked up and carried a mile before realising it's a complete piece of crap and then gets put down again. It's got this far, let's take it another half a mile and then place it on a post so the next person can carry it a bit further.'

'It'll probably get to the Meditereanean before us, the speed we're going.'

A high open valley at 2150 metres is followed for the next hour, the air crystal clear, white fluffy clouds float overhead and herds of cattle graze on green pastures, an idyllic scene . Lac Bouillouse's shores are reached and we follow a winding course through woodland for another hour, the large Refuge le Bones comes into view and is next to a huge dam. It's a sunny warm afternoon so head on up to it and order a beer or two as the day's toil is over. The sun gradually arcs around the refuge's garden, we go from one side of it to the other, being gently chased by the evening's shadows.

Thirty nine

I hear runners pass at dawn, we are camped in some trees a twenty minute walk back from the refuge on the lake's shore.

We head off early to catch the shop before lunch in the valley below. On route a diversion sends us on a detour around two lakes and over a hill before putting us on the same path we left a mile further on. I succumb to a dark mood having wasted over an hour, Jim senses my juvenile tantrum so scoots off ahead. As we drop down from the mountains, passing ski tows, new builds and chalet villages. I get a right grump on, I'm sick of walking, I'm sick of everything. I have decided to finish the walk at the next village, Bolquare. Upon arrival I see a table outside the shop which has Jim's bag on it, he's inside.

Three days' food is needed for the next section. I look at all the overpriced shelves and can't think straight, it all looks unappealing so I buy a can of beer and go back outside and drink it. It's only just after midday and the beer goes straight to my head, I try to tempt Jim into joining me but for once he is being sensible. Looking around I realise this isn't so bad after all, a lot better than working in fact so rush back in and buy just the very basics just before the shop shuts. I always buy too much food so now's a good a time as any to ration. As it happens, I run out.

The valley is broad and flat, to our right in the near distance is quite possibly the daftest border ever made. The 1659 Treaty of the Pyrenees settled two decades of fighting. Villages were to be handed to the French. Llivia and the eight kilometres around it were considered a town so remained part of Spain. So it sits landlocked as a Spanish enclave and has done for three hundred and fifty years, just two kilometres from the Spanish border. We cut across fields and open farmland to La Cabanasse, a small pretty village, quite charming in fact after the morning of ski horrors. The shop here is closed unfortunately, I sit outside waiting for Jim and think back to the last time I was here.

A storm brought in freezing rain and sleet, I sped along the wide valley to try and keep warm but the rain eventually seeped through all my layers. I was shivering uncontrollably as I arrived in the village so went into the shop to warm up and get some supplies.

A beautiful woman is shopping here also, she turns and says a chirpy 'Bon Jour' and smiles.

We stand looking at each other, I am shaking on the spot, my face is completely frozen and I try to open my mouth.

'Why wace wis wozen. Why want weak.'

She looks at me with a half smile confused and says something else in French.

I reply. 'Whym wery wold, warley voo wenglase?'

Her smile is now a frown as she realises she's just struck up a conversation with a complete nutter who makes absolutely no sense, so backs off quickly and heads to the till. Damn you frozen face! I think to myself. I buy a fresh cake as consolation.

Out of the village and across more open farmland, the GR10 then climbs up through trees to 1900 metres and a flat meadow. A long, contouring path then continues through woodland. At last craggy peaks are now directly ahead, cows mooch around us as we stick up tents in the late evening. Once more we are back in the high mountains and I'm very glad I didn't quit.

Treatment

'The brush is used lightly but still little clumps of hair come out.

'God what a sight! I look horrific. Oh well, only a couple more sessions to go.'

'What time is the appointment?' I ask.

'It's at nine thirty I have to be there, so plenty of time, I'll just put on my chemo clothes.'

Loose clothing on and a small bag packed, we walk to the hospital a couple of miles across town .

'They can't believe I walk here, they think it's great. Most people can hardly get from the car park, so I count myself lucky.'

The glass doors slide automatically open and the receptionist looks up.

'Hi Kaye, go on through. Doctor Richards wants to see you later after treatment, don't forget.'

I walk back into town, it's a cool sunny day but still mild for late November. In the centre of town a cafe does particularly good coffee so it's a good place to kill an hour. Flicking through my phone I see some clothes for auction on eBay so go to the outdoors shop down the road to see if they'll fit. I don't need them, I never really do.

At three pm there's a beep on my phone and a message comes through.

'I'll be finished in an hour.' X

The last few chemotherapy sessions have been pretty debilitating so I go back to the house and fetch the car. I pull up at the hospital, Mum's already outside and texting manically, I turn off the music as the door opens as she always has something to say.

'..So anyway, Doctor Richards said there's no sign of it spreading. In fact he said it's quite hard to see it at all...So I said to him, perhaps it's hiding behind the stent!'

' What did he say to that.. Did he laugh?'

'He just looked at me for a couple of seconds like I was bonkers.. I guess not many people joke about something when they're about to cark it.'

'You'll be alright, now it's stopped growing it may not come back for years at your age. For once being an old fart is a good thing.. When this is over, we'll do some nice things. Talking of which we'll have to get your train ticket for Christmas before they go up'

'Now that's a point... So, what shall we have for Christmas dinner?'

Forty

We pick our way up to Planell dels Bocs. The track is faint and we lose it every now and again, heading up into the high circ we pass some hunters who are sitting on a rock with rifles in hand, looking rather grumpy. I guess we may have scared away whatever they were about to shoot. Good.

We enter a high hanging valley. Vultures are in a huddle and fighting over something dead in front, as we get closer they take off, circle and land on a nearby rock. On the ground is some fur, a hoof and what looks like intestines, I expect that'll be gone soon too. A couple approach from the other direction, a pretty woman dressed like a runner in bright clothing is followed by a bearded chap in camouflage and carrying a gun, both smiling. Opposites attract and all that, either that or she's just been kidnapped.

The long curving track cuts across scree and eventually tops out at Coll de les Neu Fonts and the frontier ridge stretches out in front. For once we are on it heading over the tops and not crossing it back and forth. Pic de Nou Creus and Pic de La Fosse, big hills at 2800 metres are a joy to walk over on a twisting broad ridge. At col de Nou Creus, nine mini crucifixes adorn the hilltop. Nuria a pilgrimage complex can be seen in the valley below.

Col de Nou Creus

According to tradition Saint Giles lived in the valley around thirteen hundred years ago and crafted an image of the Virgin Mary on wood. When fleeing the Romans, he hid it in a cave with some pots. It was then found later by Amadeu, a pilgrim who had a prophetic dream. He built a chapel for pilgrims, placing in it, the cross, the found pots and the painting of the Virgin Mary. Pilgrims have been coming up ever since. Now you can arrive by train and stay in the huge hotel attached to a church and go skiing if you wish. Not so sure Saint Giles would approve.

Now once more back in Spain, the GR11 is picked up again for the last time. A thick mist then rolls up the valley, our track contours at 2400 metres below the mountain tops and becomes engulfed in cloud. The pointy peak of Gra de Fajol plays hide and seek in front leading the way to the gentle climb of Col de la Marrana. We pick a course down and join a ski run to Valter 2000.

Fajol

A lone burger stall sits by a defunct ski tow. Its flags are fluttering in the wind, the area is completely deserted, the car park below empty.

'It can't be can it?

'It is.. it's open!'

We sit in freezing thick mist waiting eagerly for our burger, it's fair to say we've failed miserably getting meals cooked for us on this trip so far. The burger is a joy and am saddened when it's gone. I would order another but the burger man has closed his hatch and is heading home.

Now re-energized, it's time to push on with a late afternoon climb up to Roc Colum. An almost dry stream bed is our last source of water for the next twenty four hours so we fill up with six litres of water each and then wobble under its weight onto a broad plateau. Mists continue to roll in and out as the path skirts the moorland slopes and arrive at a viewless Roc Colum. Continuing on, I lose all track of time and wonder if we've walked past our stopping point but underneath a rock outcrop at Porteille de Rotja, a small white cabane comes into view and is our home for the night. I took a picture of it on my last crossing. Painted brilliant white it looks an idyllic spot to spend the night.

I should have gone inside to be sure though, as the door is hanging off and rubbish is piled up inside but it would have to do. Festering blankets are put on the bottom bunk and the table cleared of rotten food and mouse shit to try and make it more 'homely'. We could of course put up the tents on some nearby flat ground but the wind is quite gusty and freezing cold. As dinner is cooked, the cloud drops to an inversion outside and a herd of cows clack past, their bells echoing as a full moon rises above.

Cabane Rotja

Forty one

It's an early start along the high flat ridge. The sun is low and bright, it outlines a guy leading a horse over rocky terrain, another horse is in tow carrying large saddlebags. I cheerfully give him my best 'Hola!' when passing. He looks up and smiles, for some reason I'm very happy this morning, perhaps it's because I didn't get bitten by a rat in my sleep.

The high ridge carries on eastwards, a rib of limestone rock adorns its back like a Stegosaurus, a white crest above sun bleached grass. Canigou is now directly opposite, it stands in a group of hills to the north. Instead of going out to it and back, a more direct route over some little hilltops seems an obvious choice, following the frontier ridge all the way to Arles sur Tech. The Spanish 1.50 000 scale map makes this look so easy. What could possibly go wrong?

As the day progresses, the gentle line of rounded hills become mountains once more, the cloud has thickened and is swirling from below and above, the sky is starting to turn a milky white. It's confusing terrain that deserves more respect than we were giving it. Now in a thick clagg, I lead us over some rocky tops, thinking the worst is over, we sit and have lunch oblivious to what lies ahead as I drink the last of my water.

Sierra Roc Negra

I look down the slope below as a gap appears in the cloud, the topography doesn't make sense, I then realise that's because we are sitting on the wrong mountain. A study of the map reveals we have headed over two mountain tops in the wrong direction. A long brooding mountain ridge runs opposite, it appears through the mist briefly confirming our mistake. That's where we should be. It's now two pm and I realise we are not even halfway. I also have no food or water left. Oops.

We double back and follow a shattered ridge that leads down into scrambling hell, crumbling pinnacles need to be traversed. It feels like untrodden ground and takes an age to find the right route to the low saddle. To reach the top of Sierra Roc Negra more heavy negotiation is needed. Sticking just below a broken ridgeline we pick a route along intersecting ledges and eventually get onto safe ground and the top. Luckily, a long thin sweeping track leads us down avoiding most of the small tops on its way. It is however, slow going and a freezing wind has picked up, the broad grassy ridge seems to be taking forever. Below, the GR10 comes into view, a steep broken path down to it just about finishes me off.

I'm delirious with thirst but there is still no water. Passing through Coll de la Cirera, old mine waste is banked up, then between some high pastures, a pipe sticks out of the ground and is spouting pure heaven. Camping around here looks like the only option as below is steep forested slopes but every square foot of flat ground has a cow pat on it. It then begins to rain, the sky is dark and wind is now blowing. It feels like a storm is coming so we abandoned any thoughts of camping in cowshit hell and head to the gite at Batra, a short walk below. The gite occupies a corner of a large building that was once the old miners accommodation, the rest of it is empty and boarded up. The gite itself is quite big but expensive so everyone staying is squashed in the small dormitory underneath. I take a long hot shower whilst Jim rustles up fish and couscous for us, as I have eaten everything I have.

We sit at the bar happily cradling a beer as the wind howls outside. The high Pyrenees are behind us and we will be at the coast within the week.

Early morning wildwest. Porteille de Rotja

Forty two

'Oh look it's snowing.'

Sleet blows across the window as we stare out from the kitchen.

'Welcome to the Mediterainean Jim.'

I eat a spare can of sardines for breakfast that Jim has carried. We need to get to Arles sur Tech before the shops shut for lunch but watching it snow outside isn't making that a very appealing proposition.

The storm keeps rumbling, it's now a mixture of sleet and rain, I stick on most of my clothes as we head out at mid morning. It's a long, dropping track to Arles Sur Tech. The GR10 follows old cables half buried, these were used by the mines higher up the mountainside. In its day, they ran for over eight kilometres for an overhead cable car system that ferried great buckets of iron ore to Arles below, quite a feat of engineering.

We pass a hippy commune complete with teepees and large veg plots, it's eerily quiet, everyone is hiding away from the freezing weather. Lower down, the heavy rain peters out as we enter town and hit the shops. The bench opposite soon becomes a battleground of food wrappers. I scoff banana sandwiches and tinned peaches with gusto and then start on a main course of avocado, tomato and crisp sandwich. Followed by a tub of grated carrots. Two french sticks later, I sit holding my groaning stomach..

Arles sits at 274 metres and is by far the lowest point for weeks, I was expecting it to be boiling down here but it's cold and damp. I can only imagine what it must be like on top of Sierra Roc Negra right now.

The campsite is on the other side of town so we start walking towards it when the skies darken again, a clap of thunder heralds more rain as we duck into a bar for a coffee. Rain continues to bounce off the pavement so we then order a beer. Locals drift in and out, tutting and shaking heads at the biblical scene outside. A chap from the insurance office next door comes in, has a shot of brandy and then goes back to his office, he then comes back at twenty minute intervals for another. He has the look of someone who does this half a dozen times a day. A couple of pleasant hours is spent before heading back to the shop to buy dinner.

We pitch our tents and decide to have another day off, Jim needs to book his bus home and I need to buy a travel plug from which we reason that this will take at least a whole day to achieve. Deep down neither of us want this to end, we have been dragging our feet of late, now they have stopped altogether.

Forty three

Montalba

Forested foothills now lay between us and the Mediterranean. Looking back from Col de Paracolls, Canigou and the Sierra Negre (eek) to the west are completley covered in snow, we made it through just in the nick of time. The route zigzags and is shaded mostly from the sun; it only gets hotter when the trees thin near the border on the high slopes. Roc de France stands on the ridgeline in front. It is topped with a great communications aerial, the view from it is no different to the rocky perch we are sat on.

'Give it a miss?'

'Yeah.'

Just below, a great beech forest covers the hillside, as the GR10 winds its way down, sunlight filters through the high canopy and shafts of light hit the forest floor. The path then arches around a ridgeline before dropping to Col del Pou de la Neu. A flat meadow in the col is perfect for camping but has no water. There's a stream marked on the map not far from here in a ravine so we head down to it. I give it little hope of running this time of year and as we approach, the stream bed is dry so we sat on the bridge above wondering what to do next.

'I think I can hear something.. Water? '

Jim scrambles down the rocky streambed for fifty metres and finds just enough of a trickle to fill up our bottles. We head back up and erect the tents. Looking out to the east the Mediteranean glints in the evening sun.

Forty four

Dropping down through pines, a dirt road gives an easy march. An old fort stands on a hillock on one corner as the Spanish plains melt away far below. Las Illas has an end of the road feel about it. Having spent an hour in Spain we are now back in France and sit in the shade of a small pension supping a coffee. A tarmac road winds it way out of the village and then dirt roads cross a high plateau of forest scrub. Small farms scrabble an existence, some looking more legal than others. We pass a naked gardener tending to his plump tomatoes, unfortunately for us, his wife in the next row doesn't follow suit. As the avenue of scrub continues, a network of dirt roads disappear into its depths. I bet all sorts are grown in there, I surmise. I'm tempted to have a look but think better of it.

This is no place to dawdle so I stretch out at a pace, it's not too hot but I want to just get this day done as it's a long one. The four wheel drive track skirts the last hillock and threads its way down off the plateau, cork trees stripped of bark line the road before entering into the mess that is Le Perthus.

Le Perthus is quite plainly, odd. One side of the road is in France the other side in Spain. The town came about via a rather bizarre border agreement which dates back to the signing of the Treaty of the Pyrenees in 1659, the same treaty that left Llivia marooned in France a few days earlier. I wasn't sure whether to say 'bonjour' or hola!.' Walking down the main street, the shops on the left were mostly selling booze and cigarettes. This was definitely the busier side, the Spanish side. The town is full of sweaty, jostling bodies pushing trolleys of liquor and beer along the narrow pavements heading back to a badly placed car park way out of town. Street sellers fill any available corner selling sunglasses and watches, anything fake in fact that they can lay their hands on.

It's all quite tardy but fun. I enjoy the spectacle whilst Jim wanders off to buy a bale of duty free tobacco. Being in a large town it is time to find a bar and sit down and have a beer, the Spanish side again, is the best option for this. There are more expensive French bars on the opposite side of the road but who in their right mind would go into one of them? We head down a side street and find a suitable hostelry. Getting a second beer we are given a ticket, a ticket still sits on the table from the first beer even though we paid for it. So when ordering a third I try to make this clear. The bar man can't make head or tail of what I'm saying so gets us another beer and throws away all the paper, charging us just for one more. We look at each other and shrug, it feels best to escape whilst the going is good, I don't think this is a town you want to upset anyone in.

The path out of town is hot and slow going, not helped by the ten beers I'm carrying in my rucksack for our final night's celebrations, so we stop and have one each. As every hour pases we stop and have another to break up the tedium. At some point the path is lost and it's getting dark, the best thing to do is have another beer and see if that will help. A road is heard just above, so a scramble up through trees and brambles ensues. Once sat on tarmac more beer is needed to help ease the pain the other beers are causing.

At last we arrive at Col de Louillat in complete darkness and camp next to a park bench. We celebrate our arrival with the last 2 beers and collapse in our tents. Drinking beer whilst walking uphill 650 metres is not to be recommended kids!

Forty five

It's slow going to Puig Neulos as yesterday's beers have sucked all moisture out of me. Mosquito bites plaster my legs. We were easy game sitting on the roadside at dusk being half cut, the only consolation being, they probably took off and crashed into the nearest tree after feasting on our blood .

Puig Neulos

Another rocket ship size radio mast sits incongruously on the hill top and drifts in and out of the mist. Scattered beech forests and pasture land are crossed as cows watch lazily. The border of Spain is a constant reminder here as a fence hangs with coils of rusting barbed wire and is followed for the next three hours. The GR10 markers are painted on stones half buried in the ground as our narrow path passes rocky outcrops sat on rolling hills. The Mediteraineran shimmers ever closer.

A bank of green hillside slowly gives way to the top and the last hill. Puig de Salfort stands at 981 metres, it gives tantalising views of coastline with Banyuls looking tiny far below and still a good three hours away. A steep path covered in shattered rock then descends the hillside and passes through vine fields, before a cruel 150 metre climb in the blazing sun crosses the last of the foothills. I am out of water but remember a font on this section of path nearby. A tree offers shade upon arrival as I neck a litre of water and start to feel human again.

A long, gravel track winds its way down, sticking to the crest of a low ridge, Banyuls is tantalisingly close just below, it feels like we're coming into land at four miles per hour. Once on tarmac, a few houses are passed before a railway tunnel spits us out and onto a succession of intertwining streets. It's fair to say, I've felt pretty odd entering a town at the best of times on this walk but Banyuls takes the biscuit. It's a hive of activity where most of the people are carrying large towels, wearing flip flops and heading to the beach. We keep walking and enter a square with a promenade opposite. I stand and stare at the wall, behind it lies a gravel beach.

All that's left is to weave a course through scattered tourists, their brown bellies poking up like mole hills and the air is thick with the smell of suntan lotion and the salty sea. Waves gently lap at my feet as my rucksack thumps to the ground behind me .

I'm instantly cooled and deafened by the headfirst plunge, the salt stings my eyes as the sea encapsulates and runs over my skin. I float looking at the sky as a rolling wave lifts and drops, its calming action gently cradles. I wonder what to do next as I wait for a euphoric moment of triumph to seize me, nothing happens, it never does.

The end never really matters as the cliche goes, it's how you get there that counts. I ponder the future and feel a moment of dread so I quickly banish such thoughts, it's better to just enjoy this moment and think about that on the flight home. I see Jim waving from the beach, two beers in hand, he puts them down and jumps in swimming over to me.

We shake hands.

'Well done Paul.'

'Cheers, the same to you, you fine fellow.. Those beers look like they're getting hot, let's go and put them out of their misery.'

Banyuls

The phone rings, I've been expecting this call and am hoping against all hope for some good news.

'Hi Mum'

'Hi Paulie'

'Well, It's not very good really. We've just looked at the scan.... 'I've got cancer in the hepatic duct between the gallbladder and liver. They are looking at options and I'm booked to see the specialist. Now don't worry, I don't want you leaving that job. We'll get through this..'

'It'll be okay.. It'll be okay'

❊ ❊ ❊

GENERAL MUSINGS

An overview.

The 'Haute Randonnee Pyrenee' (HRP), is a high level route sticking as close to the frontier ridge without the need for mountaineering. At five hundred miles long and with thirty two miles of accent it's fair to say it's no picnic. Throw in temperamental weather, high mountain passes through remote country, et voila!. You have the perfect recipe for a six week adventure.

Georges Veron walked the route in 1968 and then published the first guidebook. Where the GR10 and GR11 stick mainly to the lower mountain passes on the French and Spanish sides respectively, the objective of the HRP is to stay close to the Frontier ridge, crossing the high mountains and the border many times by following the highest paths from the Atlantic coast to the Mediteranean.

More of an idea than an official track, you can of course swap and change, use sections of the GR10 or GR11 if you'd rather. The route I followed mashed all three together so making re-supply easier and route finding, a doddle. A guide book written by Ton Josten with the catchy title of 'Haute Route Pyrenees' was the main point of reference and made life easy, as did a dozen maps.

Back in Georges' day, sections of remote country were unmarked, trackless and maps laughable (they still are). This has all changed now as blobs of paint decorate the way, a well worn groove underfoot and should you go wayward and all else fails, just switch on your phone. 'Crivens above, I appear to be in Pamplona!'

It's an amazingly varied route and there's something special about starting and finishing by the sea. As a journey you can't go any further unless you're a really good swimmer. Once underway the landscape unfolds in front of you.

The Basque foothills, when you can see them, are rolling green, the little villages are welcoming and the language is quite extraordinary. It's also an area little visited. That, combined with thick fog makes for some interesting route finding. The low, rounded hills give way to higher pastureland. High plateaus and steep sided valleys make way to a long line of successive hills now topping the 2000 metre contour line. A mountain traverse leads the way to the high Pyrenees. The gateway to these is a high, cast limestone plateau, waterless and stripped of vegetation apart from mountain pines. A complete contrast to the rich arable lands preceding it. Standing on Col d'Anaye with Pic d'Anie and Trois Rios towering either side, you have entered the high country.

The French National Park offers a steady highline, contouring below Pic Rouge with Pic du Midi towering on the horizon. The crossing of Col du Somport leads to the 3000 metre peaks Balaitous, Vignemale and Cirque Gavarnie. It's a popular area but rightly so, easy footpaths cross passes and cols at around 2500 metres.

Choice of routes can then lead to Ordesa National Park or Baroude Lakes before entering the national parks of Possets and Malandata. Barren, boulder strewn traverses of Gourgs-Blancs and Portillion lead to the slopes of Anneto, the highest mountain in the Pyrenees and also roughly the halfway point.

A quieter area is entered, as a succession of high passes and lakes follow, skirting through Aigustastortes and Marimanga National Park before entering Andorra. A highline avoids the mass commercialism of the ski industry in the valleys below. In fact, remarkably very little is encountered on the whole route. Once more into France as Pic Carlit is crossed (if you like). A final high traverse over 2000 metres above Nuria brings you down into wooded foothills. Temperatures rising and the landscape becoming more arid. Cork trees replacing mountain pines as one final pull over 1000 metre hills, drops you amongst grapevines and through to the Mediterranean sea.

Refuges or 'wine shops', as they became known, are evenly spaced throughout most of the route. At a cost of around sixty euros a day for food and accommodation, they offer lightweight travel with a bed and food but at a price.

Backpacking the route gives flexibility and is above all, cheap. Itineraries can be stretched or shortened. Having all you need strapped to your back gives incredible freedom and a good backpacking setup needs to weigh no more than eight kilograms. The drawbacks are a limited diet and carrying five to eight days' food at a time. After a week of toil and 'what the fuck's,' the pack weight becomes acceptable.

It's easy to fall into a routine on a walk like this. To bed down, far from the hoards and swim in lakes everyday to rinse and cool off. To eat fish and couscous every night and not get totally sick of it after six weeks. Tastebuds become so immune that even Refuge 'vin rouge' sold in plastic barrels is palatable. By the time you get to Lescun, it already feels like you've been living like this forever and as the Mediterranean comes into view, it's the most natural feeling in the world to wake up, sniff your armpits, shrug your shoulders and start walking .

Pack it in.

The first time I'd packed a rucksack some thirty years ago, it may as well have been glued on the floor; it was that heavy. A walking magazine I bought around the time gave helpful tips on how to approach the beast. It went something like this.

Grab the arm straps and heave the lump up onto one leg.Then swing it around (trying not to fall over) onto your shoulders. The secret is, getting the weight onto your hips. This entails bending over and doing up the waist belt just one notch short of organ failure, now stand upright again. Remember to keep your posture similar to Homo habilis or you'll fall over backwards. You're now ready to go. Enjoy!

As time went on I refined my packing. This in fact meant I just packed very little but the rucksack was still a lump. I put up with this until into my thirties, being none the wiser. Around this time the internet brought a whole world of nylon utopia into my life. The most innovative gear was from America. You no longer hankered after a tent but a shelter, a rucksack became a pack. A sleeping bag, a quilt. These became known as the big three. Sort out these items and you're on the path to (en)lightnment. From here on in, backpacking and my wallet would never be the same. I had become hooked, a gear geek and a member of Ultra Light anonymous. At first I wrote it all off. 'Nah, too light it'll fall apart'. I thought I would dip my toe in with a rucksack made from a fabric called Dyneema. 'Stronger than steel' someone one once wrote and indeed it seemed to be. I still have that bag fifteen years later. From then on, a rotation of gear has been bought and then resold on eBay. I never went down the road of Ultralight light base weights as living in Scotland, this would mean certain death but I reached a happy compromise. The gear I bought had to be light but also robust. From a pack weight of probably fourteen kilos I now carry one around seven or eight, according to airport baggage check in.

So for those who like to know such things and if you're about to walk the HRP, here's the list of what I took including the reasons why.

Rucksack ULA Catalyst.
Rubble bag bin liner.
X-Mid Tent
Zpacks 10f sleeping bag
Thermarest Neoair ¾
⅓ length of foam mat.
Leki Voyager walking poles.

The Catalyst is the largest backpack from ULA, they sell direct and do a sale run in regulation blue every so often, which is what I bought. Jason, who you met earlier in the book lives near NewYork. He has become my gear smuggler over the years whenever he flies back to England to see family, this avoids heavy taxes and postage. I took a chance on the fit and it's perfect, a great load carrier and is just the right size so that I don't have to squash the half dozen baguettes that go on top.

The Xmid is a tent that uses two walking poles to erect it. It has two porches and oodles of space without being a flapping monster in the wind. Weighing under a kilo complete, it's pretty much perfect. This again was contraband from America.

Zpacks sleeping bag. Bought second hand it has an amazing warmth to weight ratio - 1000 fill down and 800 grams in total weight, it is pure luxury to crawl into.

Thermarest ¾ Neoair, nicknamed the plank as you fall off it every time you roll over. Amazingly light and comfortable, if you can stay on it.

A piece of foam for feet when sleeping and sitting on for lunch. Folded in two and strapped to the top of the pack it also deflected the worst of the sun off any fresh food I was carrying.

Leki Voyager walking Poles - brillant knee savers. These are the cheapest ones they make but are very robust and hard wearing, having covered a few thousand miles so far.

Coldura Cone meths cooker
Ti Pot
Christmas pudding bowl and lid.
Ti spoon
Small pocket knife
Meths - whatever plastic bottle it comes in
2 x 1.5ltr Evernew water carrier
Sawyer mini water filter
3 x lighters.
2 x tough reusable carrier bags for food and above.
Spare Ziplocks, half a dozen.
Sponge and scourer
A few spare carrier bags, thin type for rubbish etc.
2 x Lucozade plastic bottles.

Coldura Cone uses minimal meths. It's just a solid aluminum

pot stand that keeps the heat in and is very light. Ti pot, great for boiling water, crap for cooking as everything burns on the bottom. Christmas pudding bowl, pour boiling water over couscous in it. Stick the lid on. Leave, eat. Also used as a mug for coffee and breakfast cereal. Fits inside the TI pot.

Small folding knife with just a blade for cutting bread, cheese, avocados etc. Wine bottles were opened using a tent peg. Grab the wine bottle between the legs in a kneeling position, push the peg downward onto the cork, this should then go into the bottle with force, a red wine facial can be the downside of this technique if applying too much pressure.

Methylated spirits are heavy so we'd split the contents of a bottle if possible. The plastic bottle that 'Alcool a bruler' (name of Meths in France) comes in, is quite soft but surprisingly robust.

I never used my water filter so sent it back. That said, there were a few occasions where it would have been handy but I survived nonetheless. Lucozade plastic drinks bottle, wide necked for easy filling from streams and slots easily into side pockets of rucksack, cost £1 with a free drink inside.

Samsung S6 active phone.
Panasonic TZ100 camera. Small CCS camera case
Anker PowerPort 15w solar panel
Anker Powercore 10000
USBs
USB plug - 2 PIn.
Black diamond Ion head torch
MP3. £10 chinese import. Takes 1 AA battery.
Spare AA's
Needle and thread.
Compass, Silva Classic
Passport holder. Euros. Credit cards.
Small wallet - Coins.

Samsung phone S6 active. Battery life was ok for a fairly old phone. It's the tough version of the S6, being drop and waterproof. I had downloaded free offline topo maps on it which even though lacking detail were more than adequate. Also used the Kindle app for books to read including the guidebook. All the usual other phone features.

Panasonic TZ100. Not a bad camera for a compact with a 25-250mm zoom. It has a one inch sensor which isn't one inch at all.. What it does have, is an incredibly complicated menu of functions, most of which are pointless. I had to factory reset the camera twice as the ISO became stuck on 500 and then blanked it out when trying to adjust it.

Anker solar panel worked surprisingly well and was the only source of power for over two weeks as my two pin plug stopped working. It would put around 15% - 20% of charge on my phone in an hour if pointed at direct sunlight. It would also charge my battery pack when strapped to the rucksack and on the move. Anker Powercore battery pack, used to charge the camera and phone. Not bad, though it seemed to lose some of its charge capacity during the trip.

Ion head torch. Takes 2 AA batteries. A good beam for walking and adjustable for use inside the tent. Had an annoying habit of not being able to turn it on when batteries were just below half power.

MP3 £10. I've had this for twelve years, a great little thing powered by a single AA battery.

Toiletries

Toothbrush
Small plastic pot of
- Toothpaste
- Anthisan
- Lanacane
- Repellent

Bar of soap
2 x Bic Orange razors

Compedes
Ibuprofen.
Couple of plasters.
Toilet roll
Deodorant.

Little plastic travel pots are great as long as you label them, brushing teeth with Anthisan isn't to be recommended..

Clothing.

Worn or carried, depending on weather.

Columbia OutDry featherweight waterproof Jacket
Waterproof trekking skirt
Montane Featherlite windproof.
Decathlon waterproof overmitts
Decathlon fleece liner gloves
Merino Beanie
North Face Cap
Sunhat; White rock
2 x running shorts with built in budgie smuggler
Running tights
Columbia Silver Ridge shirt
Rab short sleeved cotton shirt
Decathlon Merino long sleeved top, used as a mid layer
Decathlon Trek 100 padded Jacket
2 pairs of socks. TK maxx
Lightweight stuff sack
Teva Terra Fi sandals
Columbia Trans Alps FKT II trainers
Micro towel
Sunglasses

The Pyrenees are predominantly hot but storms mean the temperature can literally drop over 20c degrees in minutes. From boiling sunshine to sleet!

Most of the time I just wore the Columbia silver ridge trekking shirt, running shorts and sunhat. The shirt was great, cool to wear, dried quickly, big pockets and didn't fade. Running shorts, light, cool and comfortable, they had a built in banana hammock so there was no need for underwear. They were also used as swimming trunks. Jump in a lake and they are rinsed clean and dry in ten minutes whilst still wearing them.Other layers came on depending on the weather, or when it cooled down in the evening. I didn't take any trousers as I used running tights instead when it was either cold or wet. The padded jacket was synthetic, having used thin down jackets in the past I wanted something more useful for when it was wet. The weather was pretty good on this crossing so it wasn't worn that much. The Columbia Outdry rain jacket worked well but soon got clammy if warm, it was however, very light, the waterproof trekking skirt is basically a jacket extension to the knees. It keeps things cool and dry down below when raining.

Food.

Shopping for food in a small supermarket was surprisingly easy. To buy seven day's food the first thing you have to do is use a shopping basket. It sounds obvious but my rucksack had around a 'basket size' amount of free space for food, anymore and it wont fit, any less I'd probably starve.

Breakfast was usually 'croustillants', a very sweet granola that could also be snacked on like biscuits. Milk powder in France is extremely good and full fat. Coffee and tea, a must!
I would often boil up half or a dozen eggs after shopping. They'd just about last a week like this, eaten for snacks or sometimes breakfast. Chocolate, the cheapest normally. Nuts and dried fruit for energy. Crackers with peanut butter (when I could find it). Lunch was nearly always bread and cheese. As the days went on and the bread became stale, tomato puree was used to juice it up. Carrots. A carrot after 4 days of festering cheese is a wonderful thing and it's also almost indestructible.

Dinner was nearly always couscous / noodles with tinned fish in oil. The oil would go in the pot as well. Half a packet of soup or a veg stock cube was sometimes added as flavour.

Fresh stuff. Avocados, onions and tomatoes. The first couple of days some fresh veg and fruit for lunch is worth the weight. I love bananas but they never really stand a chance getting past day two intact. Quiches, pies, pizza slices, these would get squashed in as bonus food, if available. Food could get really boring but you're always hungry so you just ate what you had.

X - Mid

* * *

ACKNOWLEDGEMENT

I'd like to thank Sally Eathorne for the editing of this book and making sense of the words I randomly threw at the pages. Jason, for filling my life with colour since childhood. Jim, for the many laughs shared over a thousand miles and two crossings of the Pyrenees . Tom, thanks for the madness. Amanda, thank you for keeping me sane, when all around fell apart. And lastly to my Mother, who I loved dearly. She was always there for me when 'I'd balls- up yet again.' Often with a ready smile and the ability to talk the arse end off a donkey, she is and will always be greatly missed.

Oh yes. And of course to the many people in this book, who without them would have made this a very dull read indeed.

ABOUT THE AUTHOR

Paul Robertson

Traveller and general gadabout I like nothing better than being on a trail and seeing what lies inbetween. Mountains are where I feel at ease with the world and where I shall continue to explore, until my knees fall off.

https://underneaththecolors.wordpress.com/

Printed in Great Britain
by Amazon